U0892675

中华人民共和国

2017年国民经济和社会发展统计公报

STATISTICAL COMMUNIQUÉ OF THE PEOPLE'S REPUBLIC OF CHINA ON THE 2017 NATIONAL ECONOMIC AND SOCIAL DEVELOPMENT

中华人民共和国国家统计局
National Bureau of Statistics of China

2018年2月28日
February 28, 2018

中国统计出版社
China Statistics Press

图书在版编目（CIP）数据

中华人民共和国 2017 年国民经济和社会发展统计公报 = Statistical Communiqué of the People's Republic of China on the 2017 National Economic and Social Development : 汉英对照 / 中华人民共和国国家统计局编 . -- 北京 : 中国统计出版社 , 2018.3
ISBN 978-7-5037-8445-3

Ⅰ . ①中… Ⅱ . ①中… Ⅲ . ①国民经济发展—统计资料—公报—中国— 2017 —汉、英②社会发展—统计资料—公报—中国— 2017 —汉、英 Ⅳ . ① F124-66

中国版本图书馆 CIP 数据核字 (2018) 第 036960 号

中华人民共和国 2017 年国民经济和社会发展统计公报

作　　者 / 中华人民共和国国家统计局
责任编辑 / 郭 栋
装帧设计 / 黄 晨
出版发行 / 中国统计出版社
地　　址 / 北京市丰台区西三环南路甲 6 号　邮政编码 /100073
网　　址 /http://www.zgtjcbs.com
电　　话 /（010）63376866　63376907（发行部）
印　　刷 / 北京画中画印刷有限公司
经　　销 / 新华书店
开　　本 /880×1230 毫米　1/16
字　　数 /92 千字
印　　张 /4.75
版　　别 /2018 年 3 月第 1 版
版　　次 /2018 年 3 月北京第 1 次印刷
定　　价 /38.00 元

目 录

CONTENTS

中华人民共和国
2017 年国民经济和社会发展统计公报[1]

中华人民共和国国家统计局

2018 年 2 月 28 日

2017 年，各地区各部门在以习近平同志为核心的党中央坚强领导下，不断增强政治意识、大局意识、核心意识、看齐意识，深入贯彻落实党的十八大和十八届三中、四中、五中、六中、七中全会精神，认真学习贯彻党的十九大精神，以习近平新时代中国特色社会主义思想为指导，按照中央经济工作会议和《政府工作报告》部署，坚持稳中求进工作总基调，坚定不移贯彻新发展理念，坚持以提高发展质量和效益为中心，统筹推进"五位一体"总体布局和协调推进"四个全面"战略布局，以供给侧结构性改革为主线，统筹推进稳增长、促改革、调结构、惠民生、防风险各项工作，经济运行稳中有进、稳中向好、好于预期，经济社会保持平稳健康发展。

一、综合

初步核算，全年国内生产总值[2]827122 亿元，比上年增长 6.9%。其中，第一产业增加值

[1] 本公报中数据均为初步统计数。各项统计数据均未包括香港特别行政区、澳门特别行政区和台湾省。部分数据因四舍五入的原因，存在着与分项合计不等的情况。

[2] 国内生产总值、各产业增加值和人均国内生产总值绝对数按现价计算，增长速度按不变价格计算。

65468亿元，增长3.9%；第二产业增加值334623亿元，增长6.1%；第三产业增加值427032亿元，增长8.0%。第一产业增加值占国内生产总值的比重为7.9%，第二产业增加值比重为40.5%，第三产业增加值比重为51.6%。全年最终消费支出对国内生产总值增长的贡献率为58.8%，资本形成总额贡献率为32.1%，货物和服务净出口贡献率为9.1%。全年人均国内生产总值59660元，比上年增长6.3%。全年国民总收入[3]825016亿元，比上年增长7.0%。

图1　2013—2017年国内生产总值及其增长速度

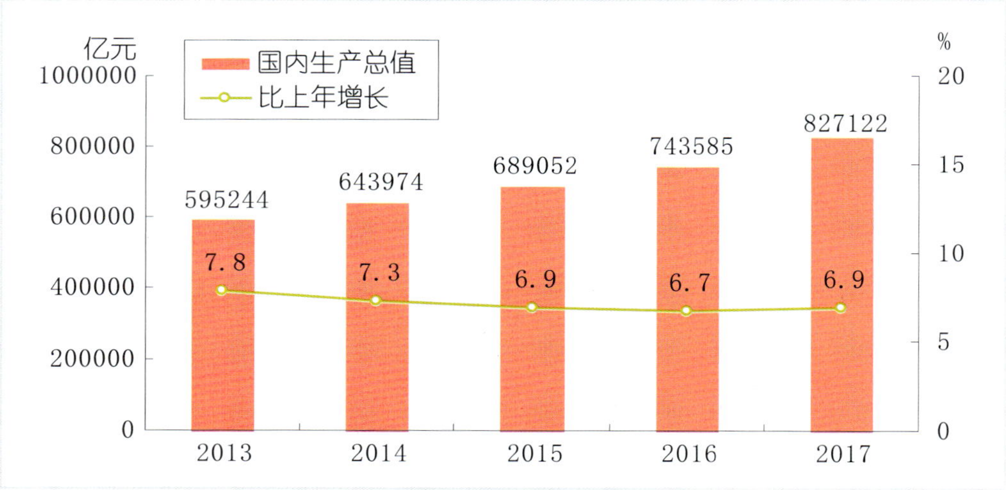

图2　2013—2017年三次产业增加值占国内生产总值比重

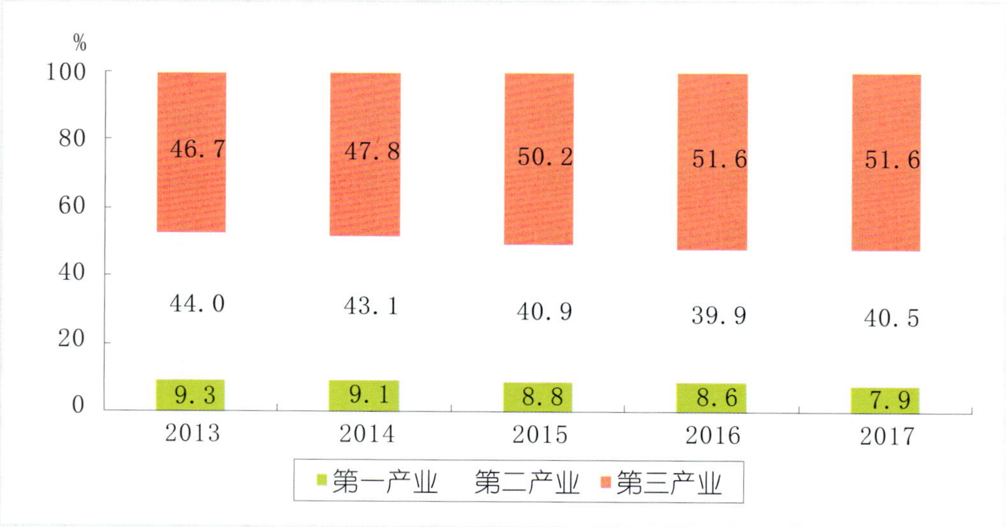

[3] 国民总收入，原称国民生产总值，是指一个国家或地区所有常住单位在一定时期内所获得的初次分配收入总额。它等于国内生产总值加上来自国外的初次分配收入净额。

年末全国大陆总人口 139008 万人，比上年末增加 737 万人，其中城镇常住人口 81347 万人，占总人口比重（常住人口城镇化率）为 58.52%，比上年末提高 1.17 个百分点。户籍人口城镇化率为 42.35%，比上年末提高 1.15 个百分点。全年出生人口 1723 万人，出生率为 12.43‰；死亡人口 986 万人，死亡率为 7.11‰；自然增长率为 5.32‰。全国人户分离的人口[4]2.91 亿人，其中流动人口[5]2.44 亿人。

表 1　2017 年年末人口数及其构成

指　标	年末数（万人）	比重（%）
全国总人口	139008	100.0
其中：城镇	81347	58.52
乡村	57661	41.48
其中：男性	71137	51.2
女性	67871	48.8
其中：0-15 岁（含不满 16 周岁）[6]	24719	17.8
16-59 岁（含不满 60 周岁）	90199	64.9
60 周岁及以上	24090	17.3
其中：65 周岁及以上	15831	11.4

年末全国就业人员 77640 万人，其中城镇就业人员 42462 万人。全年城镇新增就业 1351 万人，比上年增加 37 万人。年末城镇登记失业率为 3.90%，比上年末下降 0.12 个百分点。全国农民工[7]总量 28652 万人，比上年增长 1.7%。其中，外出农民工 17185 万人，增长 1.5%；本地农民工 11467 万人，增长 2.0%。

[4] 人户分离的人口是指居住地与户口登记地所在的乡镇街道不一致且离开户口登记地半年及以上的人口。

[5] 流动人口是指人户分离人口中扣除市辖区内人户分离的人口。市辖区内人户分离的人口是指一个直辖市或地级市所辖区内和区与区之间，居住地和户口登记地不在同一乡镇街道的人口。

[6] 2017 年年末，0—14 岁（含不满 15 周岁）人口为 23348 万人，15—59 岁（含不满 60 周岁）人口为 91570 万人。

[7] 年度农民工数量包括年内在本乡镇以外从业 6 个月及以上的外出农民工和在本乡镇内从事非农产业 6 个月及以上的本地农民工两部分。

图3 2013–2017年城镇新增就业人数

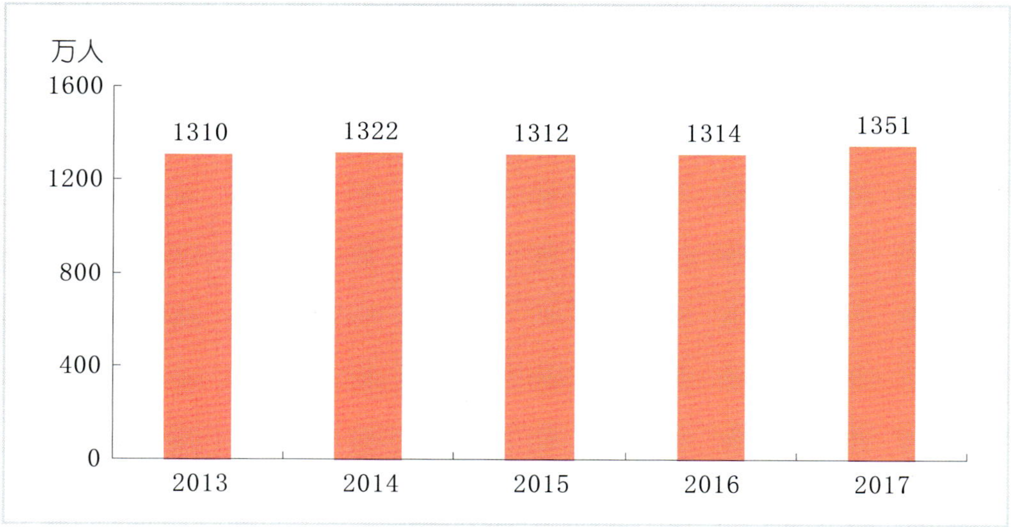

全年居民消费价格比上年上涨1.6%。工业生产者出厂价格上涨6.3%。工业生产者购进价格上涨8.1%。固定资产投资价格上涨5.8%。农产品生产者价格[8]下降3.5%。

图4 2017年居民消费价格月度涨跌幅度

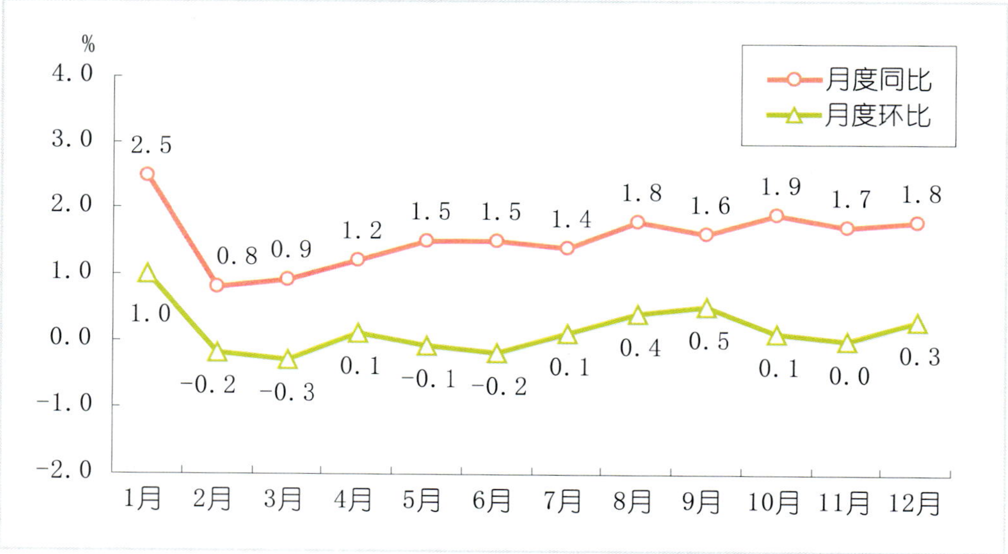

[8] 农产品生产者价格是指农产品生产者直接出售其产品时的价格。

表 2　2017 年居民消费价格比上年涨跌幅度

单位：%

指　标	全　国	城　市	农　村
居民消费价格	1.6	1.7	1.3
其中：食品烟酒	-0.4	-0.2	-1.1
衣着	1.3	1.2	1.3
居住[9]	2.6	2.5	2.7
生活用品及服务	1.1	1.0	1.2
交通和通信	1.1	1.0	1.4
教育文化和娱乐	2.4	2.4	2.3
医疗保健	6.0	6.8	4.2
其他用品和服务	2.4	2.5	2.4

12 月份 70 个大中城市新建商品住宅销售价格月同比上涨的城市个数为 61 个，比 1 月份减少 5 个；下降的为 9 个，增加 5 个。

图 5　2017 年新建商品住宅销售价格月同比上涨、下降城市个数变化情况

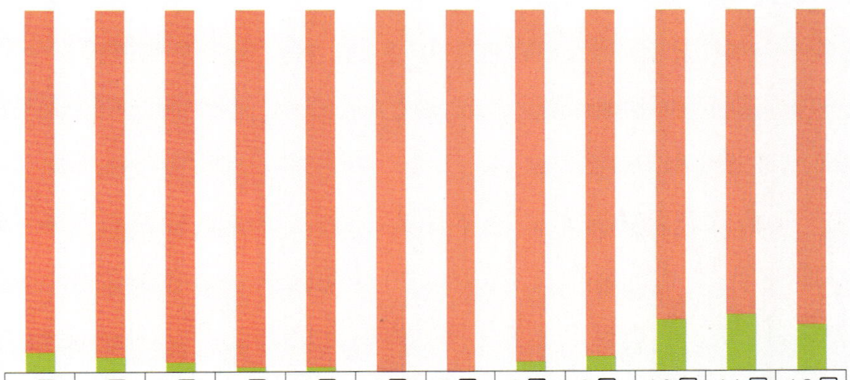

	1月	2月	3月	4月	5月	6月	7月	8月	9月	10月	11月	12月
上涨	66	67	68	69	69	70	70	68	67	60	59	61
下降	4	3	2	1	1	0	0	2	3	10	11	9

年末国家外汇储备 31399 亿美元，比上年末增加 1294 亿美元。全年人民币平均汇率为 1 美元兑 6.7518 元人民币，比上年贬值 1.6%。

[9] 居住类价格包括租赁房房租、住房保养维修及管理、水电燃料等价格。

图6 2013—2017年年末国家外汇储备

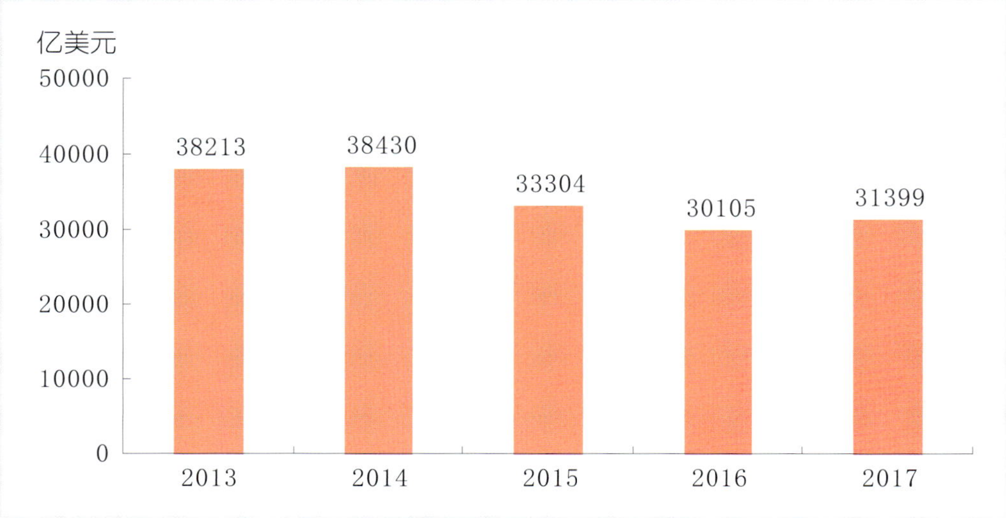

供给侧结构性改革扎实推进。全年全国工业产能利用率[10]为77.0%，比上年提高3.7个百分点。其中，煤炭开采和洗选业产能利用率为68.2%，比上年提高8.7个百分点；黑色金属冶炼和压延加工业产能利用率为75.8%，提高4.1个百分点。年末商品房待售面积58923万平方米，比上年末减少10616万平方米。其中，商品住宅待售面积30163万平方米，减少10094万平方米。年末规模以上工业企业资产负债率为55.5%，比上年末下降0.6个百分点。全年规模以上工业企业每百元主营业务收入中的成本为84.92元，比上年下降0.25元；每百元主营业务收入中的费用为7.77元，下降0.2元。全年生态保护和环境治理业、公共设施管理业、农业固定资产投资（不含农户）分别比上年增长23.9%、21.8%和16.4%。

新动能新产业新业态加快成长。全年规模以上工业战略性新兴产业[11]增加值比上年增长11.0%。高技术制造业[12]增加值增长13.4%，占规模以上工业增加值的比重为12.7%。装备制造业[13]增加值增长11.3%，占规模以上工业增加值的比重为32.7%。全年新能源汽车产量69万辆，比上年增长51.2%；智能电视产量9666万台，增长3.8%；工业机器人产量13万台（套），增长

[10] 产能利用率是指实际产出与生产能力（均以价值量计量）的比率。企业的实际产出是指企业报告期内的工业总产值；企业的生产能力是指报告期内，在劳动力、原材料、燃料、运输等保证供给的情况下，生产设备（机械）保持正常运行，企业可实现的、并能长期维持的产品产出。

[11] 工业战略性新兴产业包括节能环保产业，新一代信息技术产业，生物产业，高端装备制造产业，新能源产业，新材料产业，新能源汽车产业等七大产业中的工业相关行业。

[12] 高技术制造业包括医药制造业，航空、航天器及设备制造业，电子及通信设备制造业，计算机及办公设备制造业，医疗仪器设备及仪器仪表制造业，信息化学品制造业。

[13] 装备制造业包括金属制品业，通用设备制造业，专用设备制造业，汽车制造业，铁路、船舶、航空航天和其他运输设备制造业，电气机械和器材制造业，计算机、通信和其他电子设备制造业，仪器仪表制造业。

81.0%；民用无人机产量290万架，增长67.0%。全年规模以上服务业[14]中，战略性新兴服务业[15]营业收入41235亿元，比上年增长17.3%；实现营业利润7446亿元，增长30.2%。全年高技术产业投资[16]42912亿元，比上年增长15.9%，占固定资产投资（不含农户）的比重为6.8%；工业技术改造投资[17]105912亿元，增长16.3%，占固定资产投资（不含农户）的比重为16.8%。全年网上零售额[18]71751亿元，比上年增长32.2%。其中网上商品零售额54806亿元，增长28.0%，占社会消费品零售总额的比重为15.0%。在网上商品零售额中，吃类商品增长28.6%，穿类商品增长20.3%，用类商品增长30.8%。2016年末全国25.1%的村有电子商务配送站点。

发展质量效益改善。全年全国一般公共预算收入172567亿元，比上年增长7.4%[19]。其中税收收入144360亿元，比上年增加13999亿元，增长10.7%。全年规模以上工业企业实现利润75187亿元，比上年增长21.0%。分经济类型看，国有控股企业实现利润16651亿元，比上年增长45.1%；集体企业400亿元，下降8.5%，股份制企业52404亿元，增长23.5%，外商及港澳台商投资企业18753亿元，增长15.8%；私营企业23753亿元，增长11.7%。分门类看，采矿业实现利润4587亿元，比上年增长2.6倍；制造业66511亿元，增长18.2%；电力、热力、燃气及水生产和供应业4089亿元，下降10.7%。全年规模以上服务业企业实现营业利润23645亿元，比上年增长24.5%。全年全员劳动生产率[20]为101231元／人，比上年提高6.7%。全年制造业产品质量合格率[21]为93.71%。

[14] 规模以上服务业包括年营业收入1000万元及以上，或年末从业人员50人及以上的交通运输、仓储和邮政业，信息传输、软件和信息技术服务业，房地产业（不含房地产开发经营），租赁和商务服务业，科学研究和技术服务业，水利、环境和公共设施管理业，教育，卫生和社会工作；年营业收入500万元及以上，或年末从业人员50人及以上的居民服务、修理和其他服务业，文化、体育和娱乐业法人单位。

[15] 战略性新兴服务业包括节能环保产业，新一代信息技术产业，生物产业，高端装备制造产业，新能源产业，新材料产业，新能源汽车产业等七大产业中的服务业相关行业。

[16] 高技术产业投资包括医药制造、航空航天器及设备制造等六大类高技术制造业投资和信息服务、电子商务服务等九大类高技术服务业投资。

[17] 工业技术改造投资是指工业企业利用新技术、新工艺、新设备、新材料对现有设施、工艺条件及生产服务等进行改造提升，实现内涵式发展的投资活动。

[18] 网上零售额是指通过公共网络交易平台（主要从事实物商品交易的网上平台，包括自建网站和第三方平台）实现的商品和服务零售额。其中，网上零售额包括的服务，以及少部分用于生产经营用或被转卖的商品不统计在社会消费品零售总额中。

[19] 为推进财政资金统筹使用，2017年1月1日起将新增建设用地土地有偿使用费、南水北调工程基金、烟草企业上缴专项收入3项政府性基金调整转列一般公共预算。为此，在2016年基数中考虑3项政府性基金转列一般公共预算的影响，并以此为基础计算同口径同比增减额和增减幅。

[20] 全员劳动生产率为国内生产总值（以2015年价格计算）与全部就业人员的比率。

[21] 制造业产品质量合格率是指以产品质量检验为手段，按照规定的方法、程序和标准实施质量抽样检测，判定为质量合格的样品数占全部抽样样品数的百分比，统计调查样本覆盖制造业的29个行业。

图7 2013—2017年全国一般公共预算收入

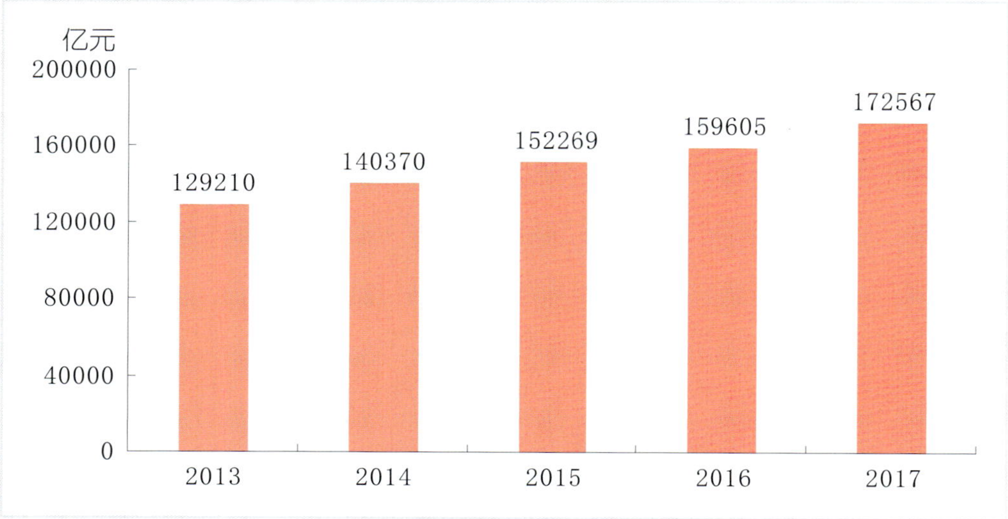

注：图中2013年至2016年数据为全国一般公共预算收入决算数，2017年为执行数。

图8 2013—2017年全员劳动生产率

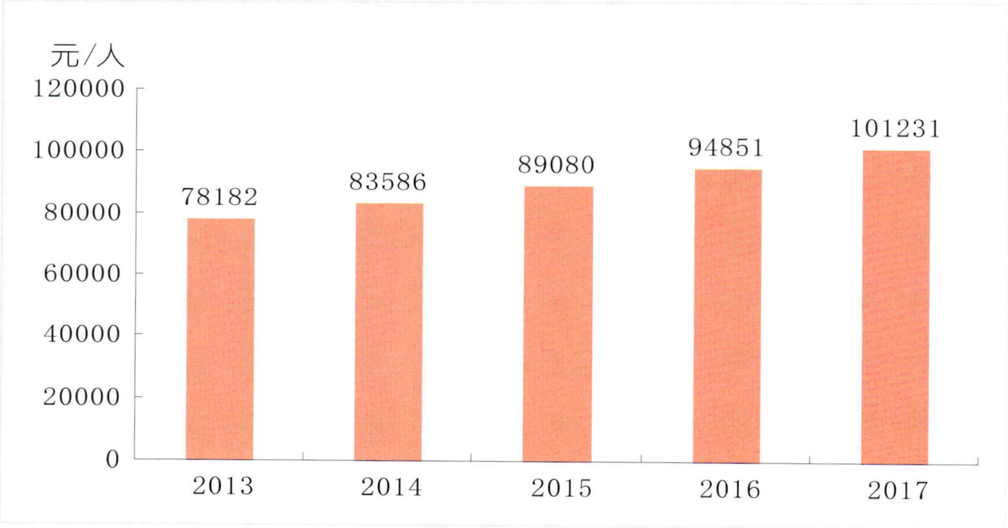

二、农业

全年粮食种植面积11222万公顷，比上年减少81万公顷。其中，小麦种植面积2399万公顷，减少20万公顷；稻谷种植面积3018万公顷，减少0.2万公顷；玉米种植面积3545万公顷，减少132万公顷。棉花种植面积323万公顷，减少12万公顷。油料种植面积1420万公顷，增加7万公顷。糖料种植面积168万公顷，减少1万公顷。

全年粮食产量61791万吨，比上年增加166万吨，增产0.3%。其中，夏粮产量14031万吨，增产0.8%；早稻产量3174万吨，减产3.2%；秋粮产量44585万吨，增产0.4%。全年谷物产量

56455万吨，比上年减产0.1%。其中，稻谷产量20856万吨，增产0.7%；小麦产量12977万吨，增产0.7%；玉米产量21589万吨，减产1.7%。

图9 2013–2017年粮食产量

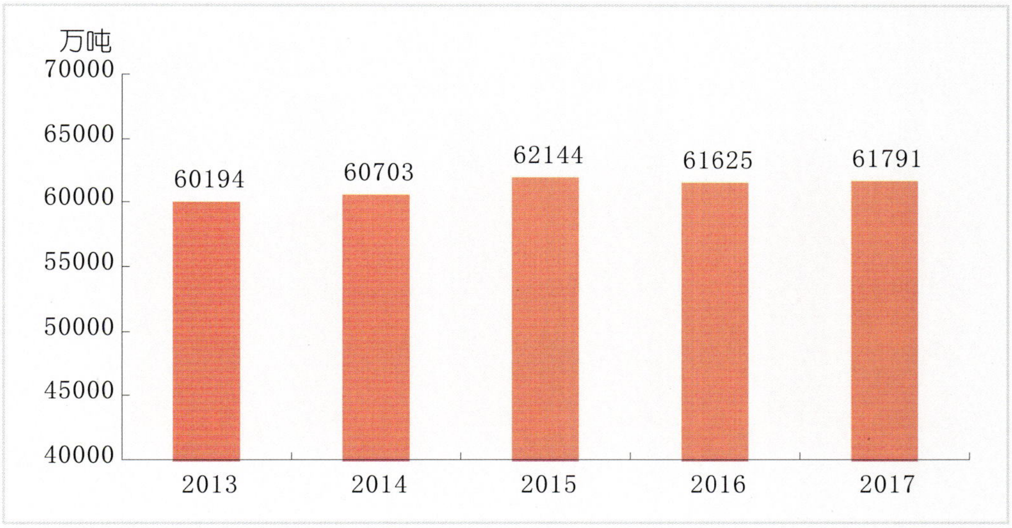

全年棉花产量549万吨，比上年增产3.5%。油料产量3732万吨，增产2.8%。糖料产量12556万吨，增产1.7%。茶叶产量255万吨，增产6.0%。

全年猪牛羊禽肉产量8431万吨，比上年增长0.8%。其中，猪肉产量5340万吨，增长0.8%；牛肉产量726万吨，增长1.3%；羊肉产量468万吨，增长1.8%；禽肉产量1897万吨，增长0.5%。禽蛋产量3070万吨，下降0.8%。牛奶产量3545万吨，下降1.6%。年末生猪存栏43325万头，下降0.4%；生猪出栏68861万头，增长0.5%。

全年水产品产量6938万吨，比上年增长0.5%。其中，养殖水产品产量5281万吨，增长2.7%；捕捞水产品产量1656万吨，下降5.8%。

全年木材产量7682万立方米，比上年下降1.2%。

全年新增耕地灌溉面积109万公顷，新增高效节水灌溉面积144万公顷。

三、工业和建筑业

全年全部工业增加值279997亿元，比上年增长6.4%。规模以上工业增加值增长6.6%。在规模以上工业中，分经济类型看，国有控股企业增长6.5%；集体企业增长0.6%，股份制企业增长6.6%，外商及港澳台商投资企业增长6.9%；私营企业增长5.9%。分门类看，采矿业下降1.5%，制造业增长7.2%，电力、热力、燃气及水生产和供应业增长8.1%。

图10　2013—2017年全部工业增加值及其增长速度

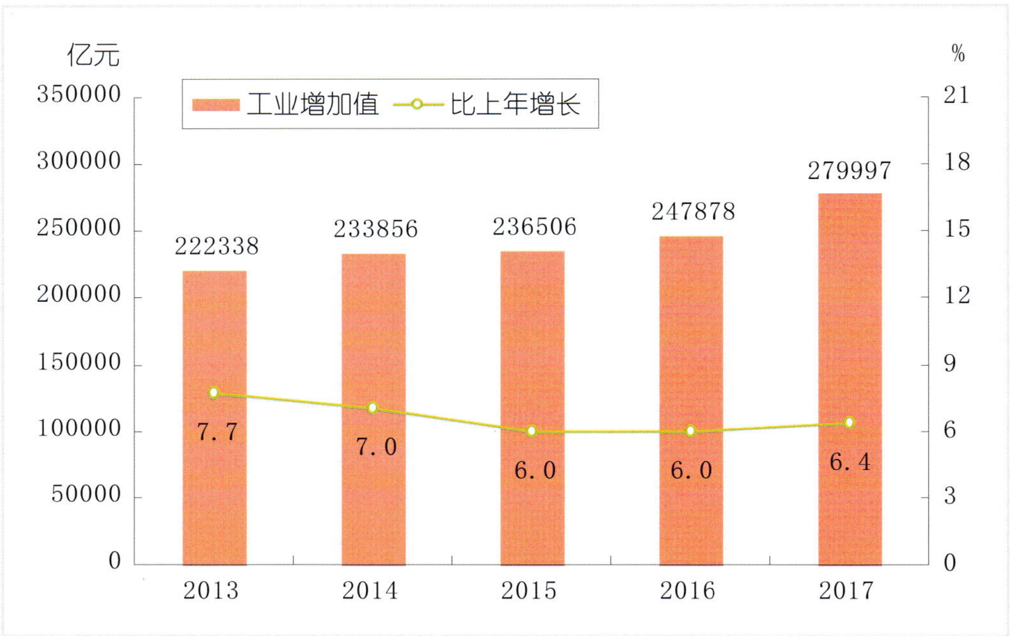

全年规模以上工业中，农副食品加工业增加值比上年增长6.8%，纺织业增长4.0%，化学原料和化学制品制造业增长3.8%，非金属矿物制品业增长3.7%，黑色金属冶炼和压延加工业增长0.3%，通用设备制造业增长10.5%，专用设备制造业增长11.8%，汽车制造业增长12.2%，电气机械和器材制造业增长10.6%，计算机、通信和其他电子设备制造业增长13.8%，电力、热力生产和供应业增长7.8%。六大高耗能行业[22]增加值增长3.0%，占规模以上工业增加值的比重为29.7%。

[22]六大高耗能行业包括石油加工、炼焦和核燃料加工业，化学原料和化学制品制造业，非金属矿物制品业，黑色金属冶炼和压延加工业，有色金属冶炼和压延加工业，电力、热力生产和供应业。

表 3　2017 年主要工业产品产量及其增长速度

产品名称	单　位	产　量	比上年增长（%）
纱	万吨	4050.0	8.5
布	亿米	868.1	-4.3
化学纤维	万吨	4919.6	0.7
成品糖	万吨	1470.6	1.9
卷烟	亿支	23448.3	-1.6
彩色电视机	万台	15932.6	1.0
其中：液晶电视机	万台	15755.9	0.3
家用电冰箱	万台	8548.4	0.8
房间空气调节器	万台	17861.5	24.5
一次能源生产总量	亿吨标准煤	35.9	3.6
原煤	亿吨	35.2	3.3
原油	万吨	19150.6	-4.1
天然气	亿立方米	1480.3	8.2
发电量	亿千瓦小时	64951.4	5.9
其中：火电[23]	亿千瓦小时	46627.4	5.1
水电	亿千瓦小时	11898.4	0.5
核电	亿千瓦小时	2480.7	16.3
粗钢	万吨	83172.8	3.0
钢材[24]	万吨	104958.8	0.1
十种有色金属	万吨	5501.0	2.9
其中：精炼铜（电解铜）	万吨	897.0	6.3
原铝（电解铝）	万吨	3329.0	2.0
水泥	亿吨	23.4	-3.1
硫酸（折 100%）	万吨	9212.9	0.9
烧碱（折 100%）	万吨	3365.2	5.1
乙烯	万吨	1821.8	2.3
化肥（折 100%）	万吨	6184.3	-6.7
发电机组（发电设备）	万千瓦	11830.4	-9.8
汽车	万辆	2901.8	3.2
其中：基本型乘用车（轿车）	万辆	1194.5	-1.4
运动型多用途乘用车（SUV）	万辆	1004.7	9.9
大中型拖拉机	万台	41.8	-32.4
集成电路	亿块	1564.6	18.7
程控交换机	万线	1240.8	-14.9
移动通信手持机[25]	万台	188982.4	2.2
微型计算机设备	万台	30678.4	5.8

[23] 火电包括燃煤发电量，燃油发电量，燃气发电量，余热、余压、余气发电量，垃圾焚烧发电量，生物质发电量。

[24] 钢材产量数据中含企业之间重复加工钢材约 24000 万吨。

[25] 移动通信手持机、钢材 2016 年产量根据有关专项调查进行了调整，2017 年产量增速均按可比口径计算。

年末全国发电装机容量177703万千瓦，比上年末增长7.6%。其中[26]，火电装机容量110604万千瓦，增长4.3%；水电装机容量34119万千瓦，增长2.7%；核电装机容量3582万千瓦，增长6.5%；并网风电装机容量16367万千瓦，增长10.5%；并网太阳能发电装机容量13025万千瓦，增长68.7%。

全年全社会建筑业增加值55689亿元，比上年增长4.3%。全国具有资质等级的总承包和专业承包建筑业企业实现利润7661亿元，增长9.7%。其中国有控股企业2313亿元，增长15.1%。

图11 2013—2017年建筑业增加值及其增长速度

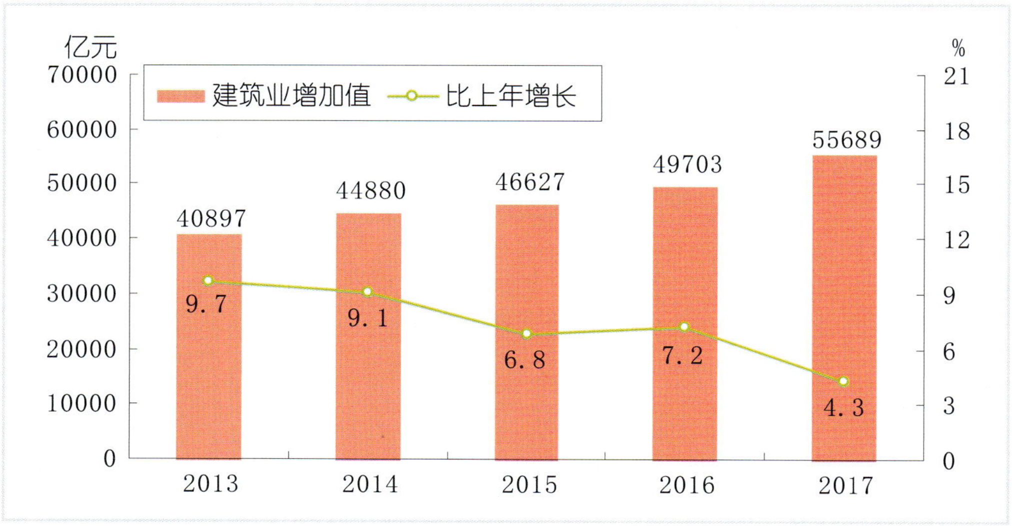

四、固定资产投资

全年全社会固定资产投资641238亿元，比上年增长7.0%[27]。其中固定资产投资（不含农户）631684亿元，增长7.2%。分区域看[28]，东部地区投资265837亿元，比上年增长8.3%；中部地区投资163400亿元，增长6.9%；西部地区投资166571亿元，增长8.5%；东北地区投资30655亿元，增长2.8%。

在固定资产投资（不含农户）中，第一产业投资20892亿元，比上年增长11.8%；第二产业投资235751亿元，增长3.2%；第三产业投资375040亿元，增长9.5%。基础设施投资[29]140005亿

[26] 少量发电装机容量（如地热等）公报中未列出。
[27] 根据第三次农业普查结果对2016年固定资产投资基数进行调整，2017年增速按可比口径计算。
[28] 固定资产投资（不含农户）按东部、中部、西部和东北地区计算的合计数据小于全国数据，是因为有部分跨地区的投资未计算在地区数据中。其中，东部地区是指北京、天津、河北、上海、江苏、浙江、福建、山东、广东和海南10省（市）；中部地区是指山西、安徽、江西、河南、湖北和湖南6省；西部地区是指内蒙古、广西、重庆、四川、贵州、云南、西藏、陕西、甘肃、青海、宁夏和新疆12省（区、市）；东北地区是指辽宁、吉林和黑龙江3省。
[29] 基础设施投资是指建造或购置为社会生产和生活提供基础性、大众性服务的工程和设施的支出。公报中的基础设施投资包括交通运输、邮政业，电信、广播电视和卫星传输服务业，互联网和相关服务业，水利、环境和公共设施管理业投资。

元，增长 19.0%，占固定资产投资（不含农户）的比重为 22.2%。民间固定资产投资[30]381510 亿元，增长 6.0%，占固定资产投资（不含农户）的比重为 60.4%。六大高耗能行业投资 64430 亿元，下降 1.8%，占固定资产投资（不含农户）的比重为 10.2%。

图 12　2013–2017 年三次产业投资占固定资产投资（不含农户）比重

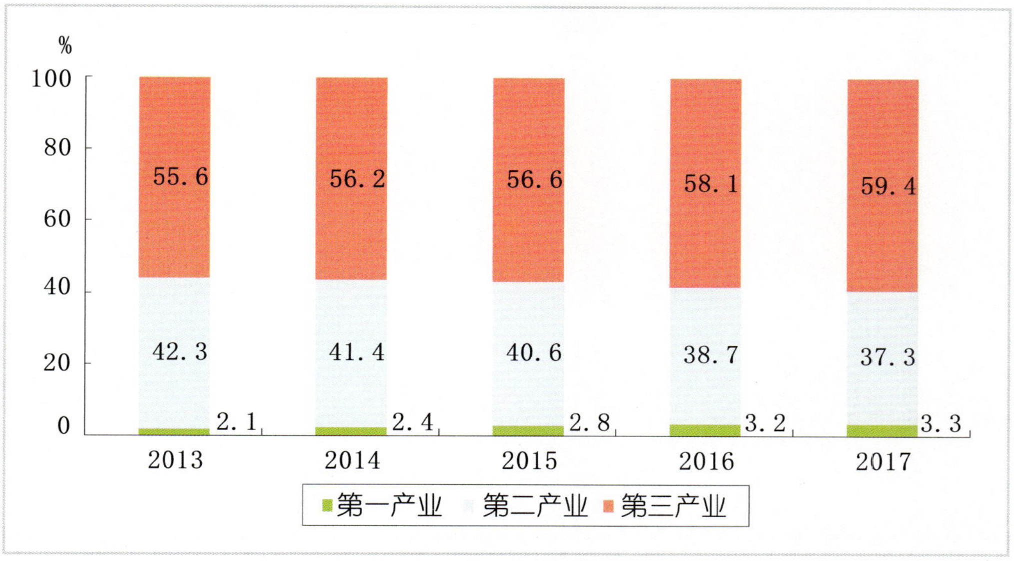

图 13　2017 年按领域分固定资产投资（不含农户）及其占比

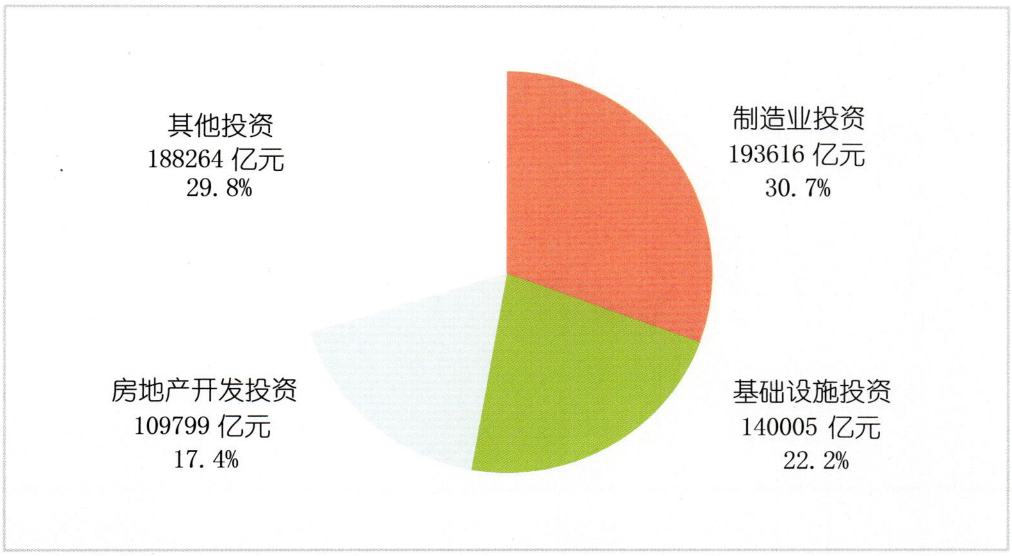

[30] 民间固定资产投资是指具有集体、私营、个人性质的内资企事业单位以及由其控股（包括绝对控股和相对控股）的企业单位建造或购置固定资产的投资。

表4 2017年分行业固定资产投资（不含农户）及其增长速度

行 业	投资额（亿元）	比上年增长（%）
总 计	631684	7.2
农、林、牧、渔业	24638	9.1
采矿业	9209	-10.0
制造业	193616	4.8
电力、热力、燃气及水生产和供应业	29794	0.8
建筑业	3648	-19.0
批发和零售业	16542	-6.3
交通运输、仓储和邮政业	61186	14.8
住宿和餐饮业	6107	3.9
信息传输、软件和信息技术服务业	6987	12.8
金融业	1121	-13.3
房地产业[31]	139734	3.6
租赁和商务服务业	13304	14.4
科学研究和技术服务业	5932	9.4
水利、环境和公共设施管理业	82105	21.2
居民服务、修理和其他服务业	2686	2.4
教育	11084	20.2
卫生和社会工作	7327	18.1
文化、体育和娱乐业	8732	12.9
公共管理、社会保障和社会组织	7931	-2.0

表5 2017年固定资产投资新增主要生产与运营能力

指 标	单 位	绝对数
新增220千伏及以上变电设备	万千伏安	24263
新建铁路投产里程	公里	3038
其中：高速铁路[32]	公里	2182
增、新建铁路复线投产里程	公里	3223
电气化铁路投产里程	公里	4583
新改建公路里程	公里	313607
其中：高速公路	公里	6796
港口万吨级码头泊位新增通过能力	万吨/年	24858
新增民用运输机场	个	11
新增光缆线路长度	万公里	705

全年房地产开发投资109799亿元，比上年增长7.0%。其中住宅投资75148亿元，增长9.4%；办公楼投资6761亿元，增长3.5%；商业营业用房投资15640亿元，下降1.2%。

[31] 房地产业投资除房地产开发投资外，还包括建设单位自建房屋以及物业管理、中介服务和其他房地产投资。

[32] 高速铁路是指线路最大速度200公里/小时及以上的铁路和200公里/小时以下仅运行动车组列车的铁路。

全年全国城镇棚户区住房改造开工 609 万套，棚户区改造基本建成 604 万套，公租房基本建成 82 万套。全年全国农村地区建档立卡贫困户危房改造 152.5 万户[33]。

表 6　2017 年房地产开发和销售主要指标及其增长速度

指　标	单　位	绝对数	比上年增长 (%)
投资额	亿元	109799	7.0
其中：住宅	亿元	75148	9.4
其中：90 平方米及以下	亿元	22367	-9.7
房屋施工面积	万平方米	781484	3.0
其中：住宅	万平方米	536444	2.9
房屋新开工面积	万平方米	178654	7.0
其中：住宅	万平方米	128098	10.5
房屋竣工面积	万平方米	101486	-4.4
其中：住宅	万平方米	71815	-7.0
商品房销售面积	万平方米	169408	7.7
其中：住宅	万平方米	144789	5.3
本年到位资金	亿元	156053	8.2
其中：国内贷款	亿元	25242	17.3
个人按揭贷款	亿元	23906	-2.0

五、国内贸易

全年社会消费品零售总额 366262 亿元，比上年增长 10.2%。按经营地统计，城镇消费品零售额 314290 亿元，增长 10.0%；乡村消费品零售额 51972 亿元，增长 11.8%。按消费类型统计，商品零售额 326618 亿元，增长 10.2%；餐饮收入额 39644 亿元，增长 10.7%。

图 14　2013—2017 年社会消费品零售总额

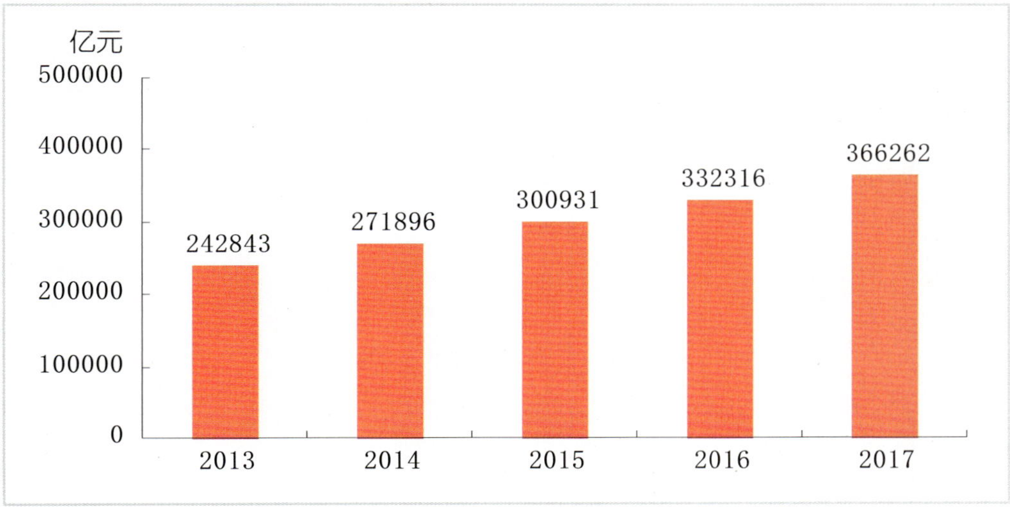

[33] 各省（自治区、直辖市）汇总上报截至 2017 年 12 月底建档立卡贫困户农村危房改造实际竣工数。

在限额以上企业商品零售额中，粮油、食品、饮料、烟酒类零售额比上年增长9.7%，服装、鞋帽、针纺织品类增长7.8%，化妆品类增长13.5%，金银珠宝类增长5.6%，日用品类增长8.0%，家用电器和音像器材类增长9.3%，中西药品类增长12.4%，文化办公用品类增长9.8%，家具类增长12.8%，通讯器材类增长11.7%，建筑及装潢材料类增长10.3%，汽车类增长5.6%，石油及制品类增长9.2%。

六、对外经济[34]

全年货物进出口总额277923亿元，比上年增长14.2%。其中，出口153321亿元，增长10.8%；进口124602亿元，增长18.7%。货物进出口差额（出口减进口）28718亿元，比上年减少4734亿元。对“一带一路”[35]沿线国家进出口总额73745亿元，比上年增长17.8%。其中，出口43045亿元，增长12.1%；进口30700亿元，增长26.8%。

图15 2013-2017年货物进出口总额

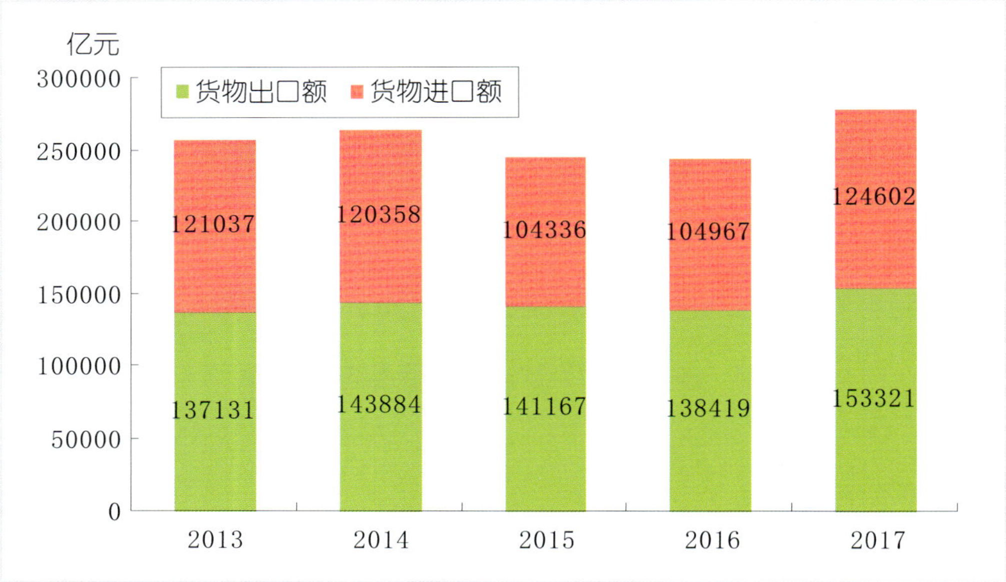

[34] 货物进出口、服务进出口、吸收外资采用人民币计价。对外投资和对外承包工程由于技术原因仍主要沿用美元计价。
[35] “一带一路”是指“丝绸之路经济带”和“21世纪海上丝绸之路”。

表 7 2017 年货物进出口总额及其增长速度

指　标	金额（亿元）	比上年增长（%）
货物进出口总额	277923	14.2
货物出口额	153321	10.8
其中：一般贸易	83325	11.7
加工贸易	51381	8.8
其中：机电产品	89465	12.1
高新技术产品	45150	13.3
货物进口额	124602	18.7
其中：一般贸易	73299	23.2
加工贸易	29180	11.3
其中：机电产品	57785	13.3
高新技术产品	39501	14.1
货物进出口差额（出口减进口）	28718	—

表 8 2017 年主要商品出口数量、金额及其增长速度

商品名称	单　位	数　量	比上年增长（%）	金　额（亿元）	比上年增长（%）
煤（包括褐煤）	万吨	817	-7.0	75	64.7
钢材	万吨	7541	-30.5	3700	3.1
纺织纱线、织物及制品	—	—	—	7441	7.4
服装及衣着附件	—	—	—	10656	2.3
鞋类	万吨	450	6.5	3269	5.0
家具及其零件	—	—	—	3385	7.4
自动数据处理设备及其部件	万台	154208	-3.1	10710	18.1
手持或车载无线电话	万台	121087	-4.8	8503	11.3
集装箱	万个	300	50.6	567	103.2
液晶显示板	万个	193367	1.6	1737	2.3
汽车	万辆	104	43.1	898	27.2

表 9　2017 年主要商品进口数量、金额及其增长速度

商品名称	单　位	数　量	比上年增长（%）	金　额（亿元）	比上年增长（%）
谷物及谷物粉	万吨	2559	16.4	440	17.2
大豆	万吨	9553	13.8	2688	19.6
食用植物油	万吨	577	4.4	307	11.3
铁矿砂及其精矿	万吨	107474	5.0	5175	35.0
氧化铝	万吨	287	-5.3	75	29.5
煤（包括褐煤）	万吨	27090	6.1	1536	63.7
原油	万吨	41957	10.1	11003	42.7
成品油	万吨	2964	6.4	982	33.3
初级形状的塑料	万吨	2868	11.5	3284	20.1
纸浆	万吨	2372	12.6	1039	28.5
钢材	万吨	1330	0.6	1027	18.2
未锻轧铜及铜材	万吨	469	-5.2	2115	21.3
集成电路	亿个	3770	10.1	17592	17.3
汽车	万辆	124	15.7	3422	16.3

表 10　2017 年对主要国家和地区货物进出口额及其增长速度

国家和地区	出口额（亿元）	比上年增长（%）	占全部出口比重（%）	进口额（亿元）	比上年增长（%）	占全部进口比重（%）
欧盟	25199	12.6	16.4	16543	20.2	13.3
美国	29103	14.5	19.0	10430	17.3	8.4
东盟	18902	11.9	12.3	15942	22.8	12.8
日本	9301	8.9	6.1	11204	16.3	9.0
中国香港	18899	-0.4	12.3	495	-54.9	0.4
韩国	6965	12.6	4.5	12013	14.4	9.6
中国台湾	2979	12.2	1.9	10512	14.5	8.4
巴西	1962	35.2	1.3	3974	31.4	3.2
印度	4615	19.8	3.0	1107	42.4	0.9
俄罗斯	2906	17.8	1.9	2790	31.0	2.2
南非	1004	18.4	0.7	1649	12.1	1.3

全年服务进出口[36]总额 46991 亿元，比上年增长 6.8%。其中，服务出口 15407 亿元，增长 10.6%；服务进口 31584 亿元，增长 5.1%。服务进出口逆差 16177 亿元。

全年吸收外商直接投资（不含银行、证券、保险）新设立企业 35652 家，比上年增长 27.8%。实际使用外商直接投资金额 8776 亿元（折 1310 亿美元），增长 7.9%，增速比上年加快 3.8 个百分点。其中“一带一路”沿线国家对华直接投资新设立企业 3857 家，增长 32.8%；对华直接投资金额 374 亿元（折 56 亿美元）。全年高技术制造业实际使用外资 666 亿元，增长 11.3%。

表 11　2017 年外商直接投资（不含银行、证券、保险）及其增长速度

行　业	企业数（家）	比上年增长（%）	实际使用金额（亿元）	比上年增长（%）
总　计	35652	27.8	8776	7.9
其中：农、林、牧、渔业	706	26.5	72	-41.6
制造业	4986	24.3	2259	-1.9
电力、燃气及水生产和供应业	372	19.6	235	68.1
交通运输、仓储和邮政业	517	21.7	374	13.6
信息传输、计算机服务和软件业	3169	116.6	1389	157.1
批发和零售业	12283	30.7	770	-23.9
房地产业	737	95.0	1133	-10.4
租赁和商务服务业	5087	9.9	1125	7.5
居民服务和其他服务业	349	42.5	38	16.0

全年对外直接投资额（不含银行、证券、保险）8108 亿元，按美元计价为 1201 亿美元，比上年下降 29.4%。其中，对“一带一路”沿线国家直接投资额 144 亿美元。

表 12　2017 年对外直接投资额（不含银行、证券、保险）及其增长速度

行　业	对外直接投资金额（亿美元）	比上年增长（%）
总　计	1201	-29.4
其中：农、林、牧、渔业	22	-25.3
采矿业	83	-4.4
制造业	191	-38.4
电力、热力、燃气及水生产和供应业	32	26.5
建筑业	73	37.5
批发和零售业	249	-9.6
交通运输、仓储和邮政业	30	-16.9
信息传输、软件和信息技术服务业	103	-49.3
房地产业	22	-79.6
租赁和商务服务业	349	-17.3

[36] 服务进出口按照《国际收支手册（第六版）》标准统计，增速按可比口径计算。

全年对外承包工程业务完成营业额11383亿元，按美元计价为1686亿美元，比上年增长5.8%。其中，对“一带一路”沿线国家完成营业额855亿美元，增长12.6%，占对外承包工程业务完成营业额比重为50.7%。对外劳务合作派出各类劳务人员52万人，增长5.7%。

七、交通、邮电和旅游

全年货物运输总量479亿吨，比上年增长9.3%。货物运输周转量196130亿吨公里，增长5.1%。全年规模以上港口完成货物吞吐量126亿吨，比上年增长6.4%，其中外贸货物吞吐量40亿吨，增长5.7%。规模以上港口集装箱吞吐量23680万标准箱，增长8.3%。

表13 2017年各种运输方式完成货物运输量及其增长速度

指　标	单　位	绝对数	比上年增长（%）
货物运输总量	**亿吨**	**479.4**	**9.3**
铁　路	亿吨	36.9	10.7
公　路	亿吨	368.0	10.1
水　运	亿吨	66.6	4.3
民　航	万吨	705.8	5.7
管　道	亿吨	7.9	7.3
货物运输周转量	**亿吨公里**	**196130.4**	**5.1**
铁　路	亿吨公里	26962.2	13.3
公　路	亿吨公里	66712.5	9.2
水　运	亿吨公里	97455.0	0.1
民　航	亿吨公里	243.5	9.5
管　道	亿吨公里	4757.2	13.4

全年旅客运输总量185亿人次，比上年下降2.6%。旅客运输周转量32813亿人公里，增长5.0%。

表14 2017年各种运输方式完成旅客运输量及其增长速度

指　标	单　位	绝对数	比上年增长（%）
旅客运输总量	**亿人次**	**185.1**	**-2.6**
铁　路	亿人次	30.8	9.6
公　路	亿人次	145.9	-5.4
水　运	亿人次	2.8	4.1
民　航	亿人次	5.5	13.0
旅客运输周转量	**亿人公里**	**32812.7**	**5.0**
铁　路	亿人公里	13456.9	7.0
公　路	亿人公里	9765.1	-4.5
水　运	亿人公里	77.9	7.7
民　航	亿人公里	9512.8	13.5

年末全国民用汽车保有量21743万辆（包括三轮汽车和低速货车820万辆），比上年末增

长 11.8%，其中私人汽车保有量 18695 万辆，增长 12.9%。民用轿车保有量 12185 万辆，增长 12.0%，其中私人轿车 11416 万辆，增长 12.5%。

全年完成邮政行业业务总量[37]9764 亿元，比上年增长 32.0%。邮政业全年完成邮政函件业务 31.5 亿件，包裹业务 0.3 亿件，快递业务量 400.6 亿件；快递业务收入 4957 亿元。全年完成电信业务总量[38]27557 亿元，比上年增长 76.4%。电信业全年新增移动电话交换机容量[39]23646 万户，达到 242186 万户。年末全国电话用户总数 161125 万户，其中移动电话用户 141749 万户。移动电话普及率上升至 102.5 部／百人。固定互联网宽带接入用户[40]34854 万户，比上年增加 5133 万户，其中固定互联网光纤宽带接入用户[41]29392 万户，比上年增加 6627 万户；移动宽带用户[42]113152 万户，增加 19077 万户。移动互联网接入流量 246 亿 G，比上年增长 162.7%。互联网上网人数 7.72 亿人，增加 4074 万人，其中手机上网人数[43]7.53 亿人，增加 5734 万人。互联网普及率达到 55.8%，其中农村地区互联网普及率达到 35.4%。软件和信息技术服务业[44]完成软件业务收入 55037 亿元，比上年增长 13.9%。

图 16　2013—2017 年快递业务量及其增长速度

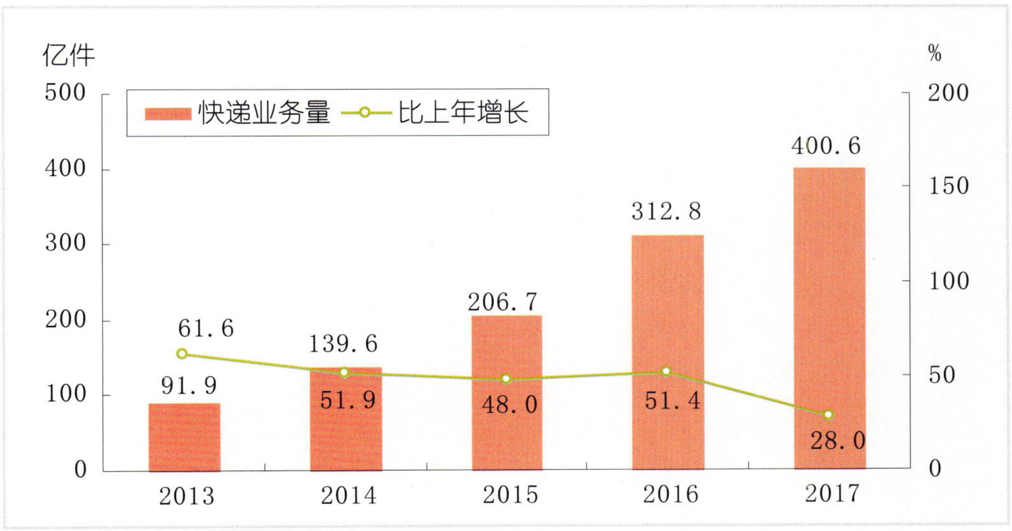

[37] 邮政行业业务总量按 2010 年价格计算。

[38] 电信业务总量按 2015 年价格计算。

[39] 移动电话交换机容量是指移动电话交换机根据一定话务模型和交换机处理能力计算出来的最大同时服务用户的数量。

[40] 固定互联网宽带接入用户是指报告期末在电信企业登记注册，通过 xDSL、FTTx+LAN、FTTH/O 以及其他宽带接入方式和普通专线接入公众互联网的用户。

[41] 固定互联网光纤宽带接入用户是指报告期末在电信企业登记注册，通过 FTTH 或 FTTO 方式接入公众互联网的用户。

[42] 移动宽带用户是指报告期末在计费系统拥有使用信息，占用 3G 或 4G 网络资源的在网用户。

[43] 手机上网人数是指过去半年通过手机接入并使用互联网的 6 周岁及以上中国居民数量。

[44] 软件和信息技术服务业包括软件开发，信息系统集成服务，信息技术咨询服务，数据处理和存储服务，集成电路设计和其他信息技术服务等行业。

图17 2013–2017年年末固定互联网宽带接入用户和移动宽带用户数

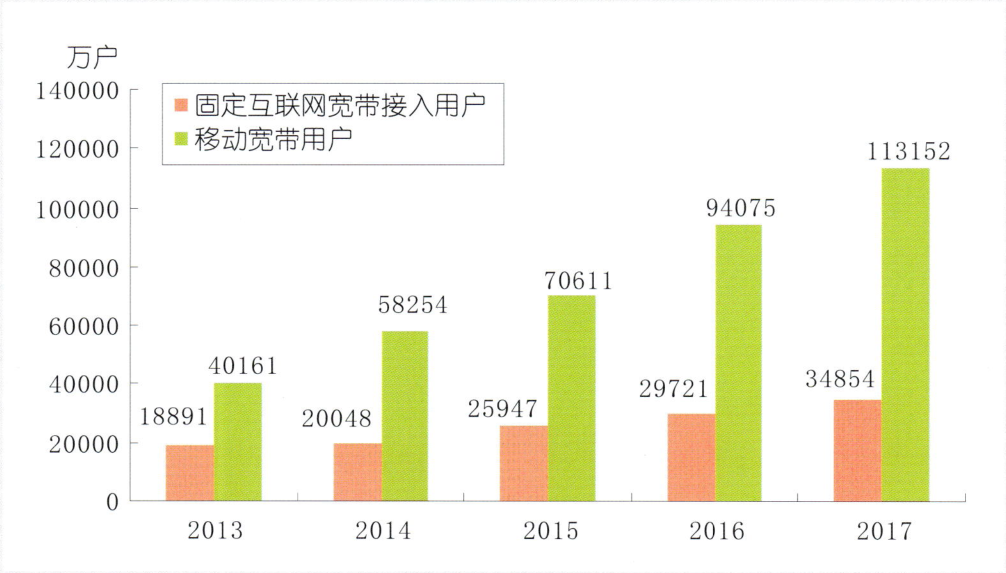

全年国内游客50亿人次，比上年增长12.8%；国内旅游收入45661亿元，增长15.9%。入境游客13948万人次，增长0.8%。其中，外国人2917万人次，增长3.6%；香港、澳门和台湾同胞11032万人次，与上年持平。在入境游客中，过夜游客6074万人次，增长2.5%。国际旅游收入1234亿美元，增长2.9%。国内居民出境14273万人次，增长5.6%。其中因私出境13582万人次，增长5.7%；赴港澳台出境8698万人次，增长3.6%。

八、金融

年末广义货币供应量（M_2）余额167.7万亿元，比上年末增长8.2%；狭义货币供应量（M_1）余额54.4万亿元，增长11.8%；流通中货币（M_0）余额7.1万亿元，增长3.4%。

全年社会融资规模增量[45]19.4万亿元，按可比口径计算比上年多1.6万亿元；年末社会融资规模存量[46]174.6万亿元，比上年末增长12.0%。年末全部金融机构本外币各项存款余额169.3万亿元，比年初增加13.7万亿元，其中人民币各项存款余额164.1万亿元，增加13.5万亿元。全部金融机构本外币各项贷款余额125.6万亿元，增加13.6万亿元，其中人民币各项贷款余额120.1万亿元，增加13.5万亿元。

[45]社会融资规模增量是指一定时期内实体经济（境内非金融企业和个人）从金融体系获得的资金总额。

[46]社会融资规模存量是指一定时期末（月末、季末或年末）实体经济（境内非金融企业和个人）从金融体系获得的资金余额。

表 15　2017 年年末全部金融机构本外币存贷款余额及其增长速度

指　标	年末数（亿元）	比上年末增长（%）
各项存款	1692727	8.8
其中：境内住户存款	651983	7.5
其中：人民币	643768	7.7
境内非金融企业存款	571641	7.7
各项贷款	1256074	12.1
其中：境内短期贷款	411153	8.2
境内中长期贷款	750894	18.2

年末主要农村金融机构（农村信用社、农村合作银行、农村商业银行）人民币贷款余额 149820 亿元，比年初增加 15602 亿元。全部金融机构人民币消费贷款余额 315194 亿元，增加 64717 亿元。其中，个人短期消费贷款余额 68041 亿元，增加 18724 亿元；个人中长期消费贷款余额 247154 亿元，增加 45993 亿元。

全年上市公司通过境内市场累计筹资 40836 亿元，比上年减少 12244 亿元。其中，首次公开发行 A 股完成申购 419 只，筹资 2186 亿元；A 股现金再融资（包括公开增发、定向增发、配股、优先股）9209 亿元，减少 4178 亿元；上市公司通过沪深交易所发行债券（包括公司债、可转债、可交换债和企业资产支持证券）筹资 28105 亿元，减少 8563 亿元。全年全国中小企业股份转让系统[47]新增挂牌公司 2176 家，筹资 1336 亿元，减少 3.95%。

全年发行公司信用类债券[48]5.64 万亿元，比上年减少 2.59 万亿元。

全年保险公司原保险保费收入[49]36581 亿元，比上年增长 18.2%。其中，寿险业务原保险保费收入 21456 亿元，健康险和意外伤害险业务原保险保费收入 5291 亿元，财产险业务原保险保费收入 9835 亿元。支付各类赔款及给付 11181 亿元。其中，寿险业务给付 4575 亿元，健康险和意外伤害险赔款及给付 1518 亿元，财产险业务赔款 5087 亿元。

九、居民收入消费和社会保障

全年全国居民人均可支配收入[50]25974 元，比上年增长 9.0%，扣除价格因素，实际增长 7.3%。

[47] 全国中小企业股份转让系统又称“新三板”，是 2012 年经国务院批准设立的全国性证券交易场所。

[48] 公司信用类债券包括非金融企业债务融资工具、企业债券以及公司债、可转债等。

[49] 原保险保费收入是指保险企业确认的原保险合同保费收入。

[50] 全国居民收入名义增速快于分城乡居民收入增速的原因是：在城镇化过程中，一部分在农村收入较高的人口进入城镇地区，但在城镇属于较低收入人群，他们的迁移对城乡居民收入均有拉低作用。但无论在城镇还是农村，其收入增长效应都会体现在全体居民收入增长中。

全国居民人均可支配收入中位数[51]22408元，增长7.3%。按常住地分，城镇居民人均可支配收入36396元，比上年增长8.3%，扣除价格因素，实际增长6.5%。城镇居民人均可支配收入中位数33834元，增长7.2%。农村居民人均可支配收入13432元，比上年增长8.6%，扣除价格因素，实际增长7.3%。农村居民人均可支配收入中位数11969元，增长7.4%。按全国居民五等份收入分组[52]，低收入组人均可支配收入5958元，中等偏下收入组人均可支配收入13843元，中等收入组人均可支配收入22495元，中等偏上收入组人均可支配收入34547元，高收入组人均可支配收入64934元。全国农民工人均月收入3485元，比上年增长6.4%。

全国居民人均消费支出18322元，比上年增长7.1%，扣除价格因素，实际增长5.4%。按常住地分，城镇居民人均消费支出24445元，增长5.9%，扣除价格因素，实际增长4.1%；农村居民人均消费支出10955元，增长8.1%，扣除价格因素，实际增长6.8%。恩格尔系数为29.3%，比上年下降0.8个百分点，其中城镇为28.6%，农村为31.2%。

图18　2013—2017年全国居民人均可支配收入及其增长速度

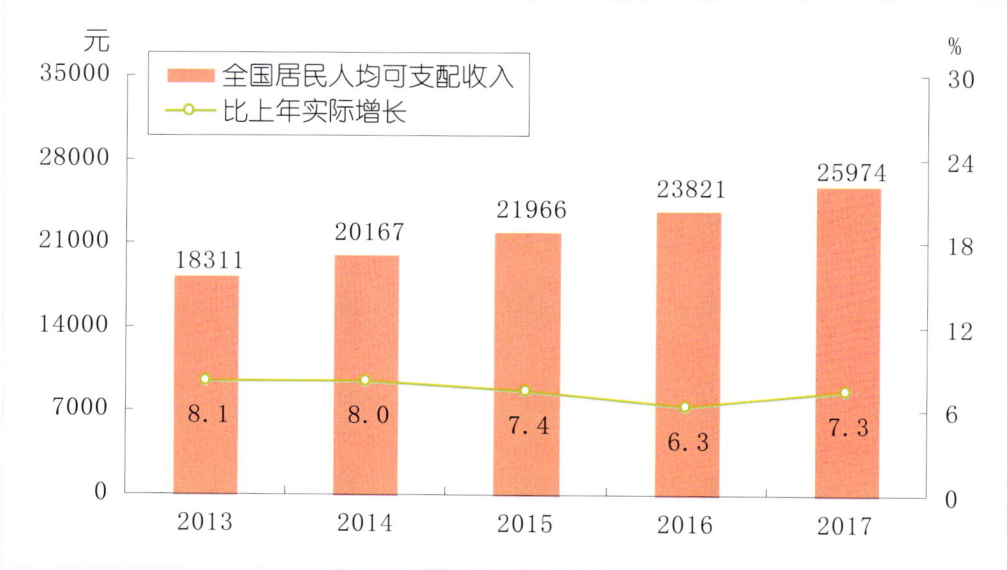

[51] 人均收入中位数是指将所有调查户按人均收入水平从低到高（或从高到低）顺序排列，处于最中间位置调查户的人均收入。

[52] 全国居民五等份收入分组是指将所有调查户按人均收入水平从高到低顺序排列，平均分为五个等份，处于最高20%的收入群体为高收入组，依此类推依次为中等偏上收入组、中等收入组、中等偏下收入组、低收入组。

图 19　2017 年全国居民人均消费支出及其构成

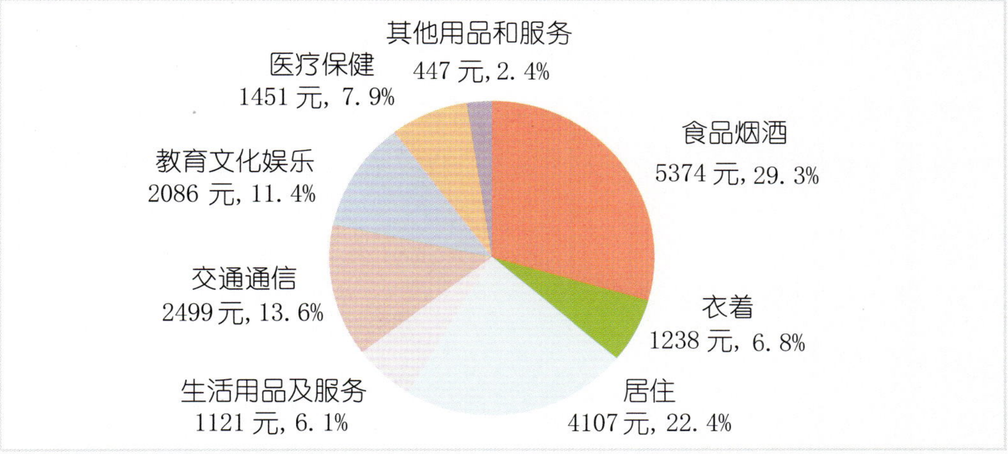

按照每人每年 2300 元（2010 年不变价）的农村贫困标准计算，2017 年，年末农村贫困人口 3046 万人，比上年末减少 1289 万人[53]；贫困发生率[54]3.1%，比上年下降 1.4 个百分点。贫困地区[55]农村居民人均可支配收入 9377 元，比上年增长 10.5%，扣除价格因素，实际增长 9.1%。

图 20　2013—2017 年年末全国农村贫困人口

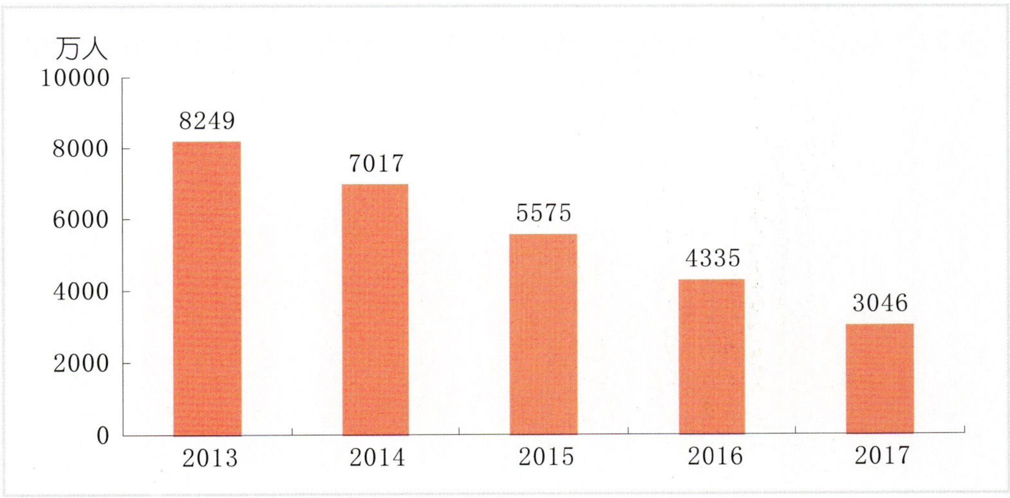

年末全国参加城镇职工基本养老保险人数 40199 万人，比上年末增加 2269 万人。参加城乡居民基本养老保险人数 51255 万人，增加 408 万人。参加基本医疗保险人数 117664 万人，增加 43272 万人。其中，参加职工基本医疗保险人数 30320 万人，增加 789 万人；参加城乡居民基本医疗保险

[53] 减贫人口等于当年贫困人口减去上年贫困人口，也相当于当年脱贫人口减去当年返贫人口。
[54] 贫困发生率是指贫困人口占目标调查人口的比重。
[55] 贫困地区包括集中连片特困地区和片区外的国家扶贫开发工作重点县，原共有 832 个县。2017 年开始将新疆阿克苏地区纳入贫困监测范围。

人数87343万人[56]，增加42483万人。参加失业保险人数18784万人，增加695万人。年末全国领取失业保险金人数220万人。参加工伤保险人数22726万人，增加836万人，其中参加工伤保险的农民工7807万人，增加297万人。参加生育保险人数19240万人，增加789万人。年末全国共有1264万人享受城市居民最低生活保障，4047万人享受农村居民最低生活保障，467万人享受农村特困人员[57]救助供养。全年资助5203万人参加基本医疗保险，医疗救助3536万人次。国家抚恤、补助各类优抚对象859万人。

十、教育、科学技术和文化体育

全年研究生教育[58]招生80.5万人，在学研究生263.9万人，毕业生57.8万人。普通本专科招生761.5万人，在校生2753.6万人，毕业生735.8万人。中等职业教育[59]招生582.4万人，在校生1592.5万人，毕业生496.9万人。普通高中招生800.1万人，在校生2374.5万人，毕业生775.7万人。初中招生1547.2万人，在校生4442.1万人，毕业生1397.5万人。普通小学招生1766.6万人，在校生10093.7万人，毕业生1565.9万人。特殊教育招生11.1万人，在校生57.9万人，毕业生6.9万人。学前教育在园幼儿4600.1万人。九年义务教育巩固率为93.8%，高中阶段毛入学率为88.3%。

图21 2013–2017年普通本专科、中等职业教育及普通高中招生人数

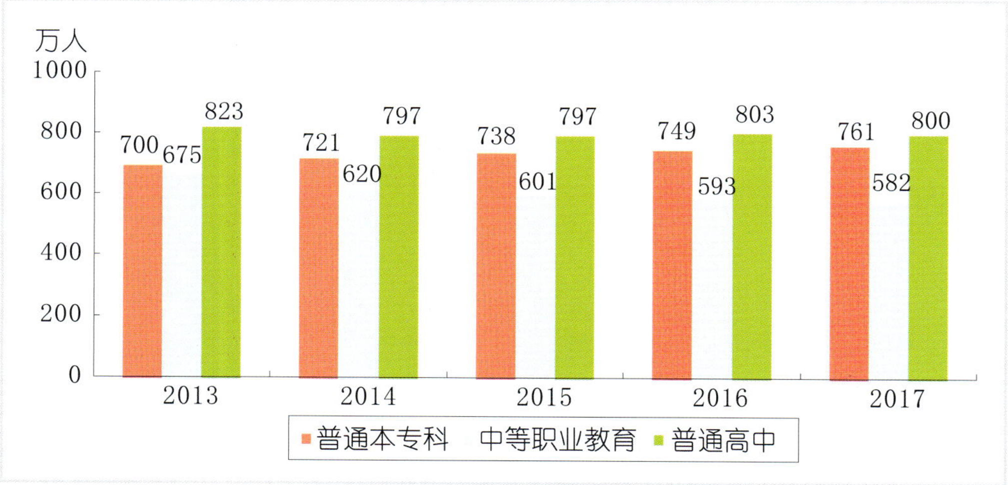

[56] 参加城乡居民基本医疗保险人数增加较多，一是原参加新型农村合作医疗人员并入城乡居民基本医疗保险参保人员统计；二是开展全民参保登记，基本医疗保险覆盖面进一步扩大。

[57] 农村特困人员是指无劳动能力，无生活来源，无法定赡养、抚养、扶养义务人或者其法定义务人无履行义务能力的农村老年人、残疾人以及未满16周岁的未成年人。

[58]2017年研究生招生、在学研究生指标口径发生变化（增加非全日制研究生）。

[59] 中等职业教育包括普通中专、成人中专、职业高中和技工学校。

全年研究与试验发展（R&D）经费支出 17500 亿元，比上年增长 11.6%，与国内生产总值之比为 2.12%，其中基础研究经费 920 亿元。全年国家重点研发计划共安排 42 个重点专项 1115 个科技项目，国家科技重大专项共安排 454 个课题，国家自然科学基金共资助 43935 个项目。截至年底，累计建设国家重点实验室 503 个，国家工程研究中心 131 个，国家工程实验室 217 个，国家企业技术中心 1276 家。国家科技成果转化引导基金累计设立 5 支子基金，资金总规模 247.2 亿元。全年境内外专利申请 369.8 万件，授予专利权 183.6 万件；PCT 专利申请受理量[60]为 5.1 万件。截至年底，有效专利 714.8 万件，其中境内有效发明专利 135.6 万件，每万人口发明专利拥有量 9.8 件。全年共签订技术合同 36.8 万项，技术合同成交金额 13424 亿元，比上年增长 17.7%。

图 22　2013–2017 年研究与试验发展（R&D）经费支出及其增长速度

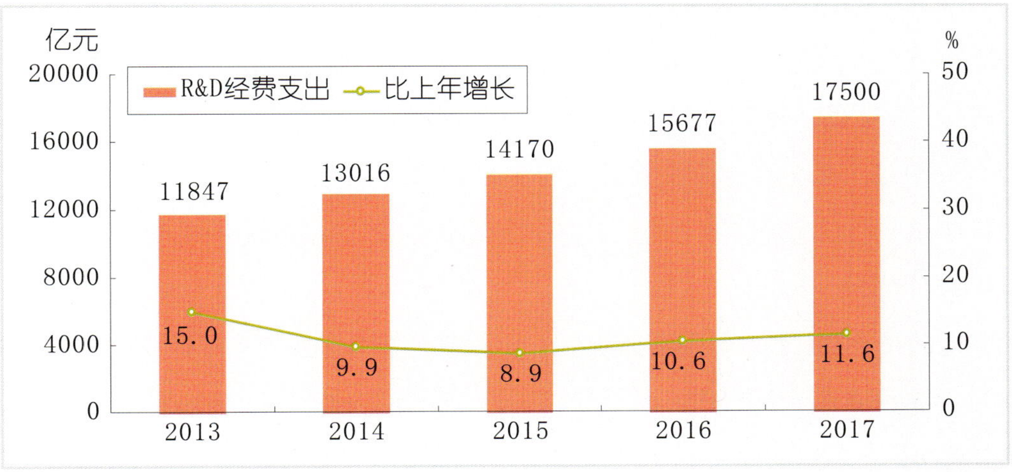

表 16　2017 年专利申请、授权和有效专利情况

指　标	专利数（万件）
专利申请数	**369.8**
其中：境内专利申请	351.3
其中：发明专利申请	138.2
其中：境内发明专利	123.4
专利授权数	**183.6**
其中：境内专利授权	170.5
其中：发明专利授权	42.0
其中：境内发明专利	32.0
年末有效专利数	**714.8**
其中：境内有效专利	620.4
其中：有效发明专利	208.5
其中：境内有效发明专利	135.6

[60]PCT 专利申请受理量是指国家知识产权局作为 PCT 专利申请受理局受理的 PCT 专利申请数量。PCT(Patent Cooperation Treaty) 即专利合作条约，是专利领域的一项国际合作条约。

全年成功完成17次宇航发射。首颗高轨道高通量通信卫星实践十三号、首颗大型硬X射线空间探测卫星“慧眼”卫星成功发射；北斗导航全球卫星系统组网首发双星成功发射；天舟一号货运飞船成功发射，完成与天宫二号交会对接。“墨子号”量子卫星成功实现预定科学目标，暗物质粒子探测卫星“悟空”发现反常电子信号，C919大型客机、“鲲龙”AG600水陆两栖飞机首飞成功。

年末全国共有产品检测实验室35000个，其中国家检测中心739个。全国现有产品质量、体系认证机构401个，已累计完成对140250个企业的产品认证。全国共有法定计量技术机构4037个，全年强制检定计量器具8326万台（件）。全年制定、修订国家标准3811项，其中新制定2684项。

年末全国文化系统共有艺术表演团体2054个，博物馆3217个。全国共有公共图书馆3162个，总流通[61]72641万人次；文化馆3327个。有线电视实际用户2.20亿户，其中有线数字电视实际用户1.98亿户。年末广播节目综合人口覆盖率为98.7%，电视节目综合人口覆盖率为99.1%。全年生产电视剧310部13310集，电视动画片83599分钟。全年生产故事影片798部，科教、纪录、动画和特种影片[62]172部。出版各类报纸368亿份，各类期刊26亿册，图书90亿册（张），人均图书拥有量[63]6.49册（张）。年末全国共有档案馆4237个，已开放各类档案13806万卷（件）。2016年，文化及相关产业增加值30785亿元，比上年增长13.0%；占国内生产总值的比重为4.14%，比上年提高0.19个百分点。

全年我国运动员在24个运动大项中获得106个世界冠军，共创6项世界纪录。全年我国残疾人运动员在11项国际赛事中获得160个世界冠军。2016年，体育产业增加值6475亿元，比上年增长17.8%；占国内生产总值的比重为0.9%，比上年提高0.1个百分点。

十一、卫生和社会服务

年末全国共有医疗卫生机构99.5万个，其中医院3.0万个，在医院中有公立医院1.2万个，民营医院1.8万个；基层医疗卫生机构94.0万个，其中乡镇卫生院3.7万个，社区卫生服务中心（站）3.5万个，门诊部（所）23.0万个，村卫生室63.8万个；专业公共卫生机构2.2万个，其中疾病预防控制中心3482个，卫生监督所（中心）3133个。年末卫生技术人员891万人，其中执业医师和执业助理医师335万人，注册护士379万人。医疗卫生机构床位785万张，其中医院609万张，

[61]总流通人次是指本年度内到图书馆场馆接受图书馆服务的总人次，包括借阅书刊、咨询问题以及参加各类读者活动等。

[62]特种影片是指那些采用与常规影院放映在技术、设备、节目方面不同的电影展示方式，如巨幕电影、立体电影、立体特效（4D）电影、动感电影、球幕电影等。

[63]人均图书拥有量是指在一年内全国平均每人能拥有的当年出版图书册数。

乡镇卫生院 125 万张。全年总诊疗人次[64]81.0 亿人次，出院人数[65]2.4 亿人。

图 23　2013–2017 年年末卫生技术人员人数

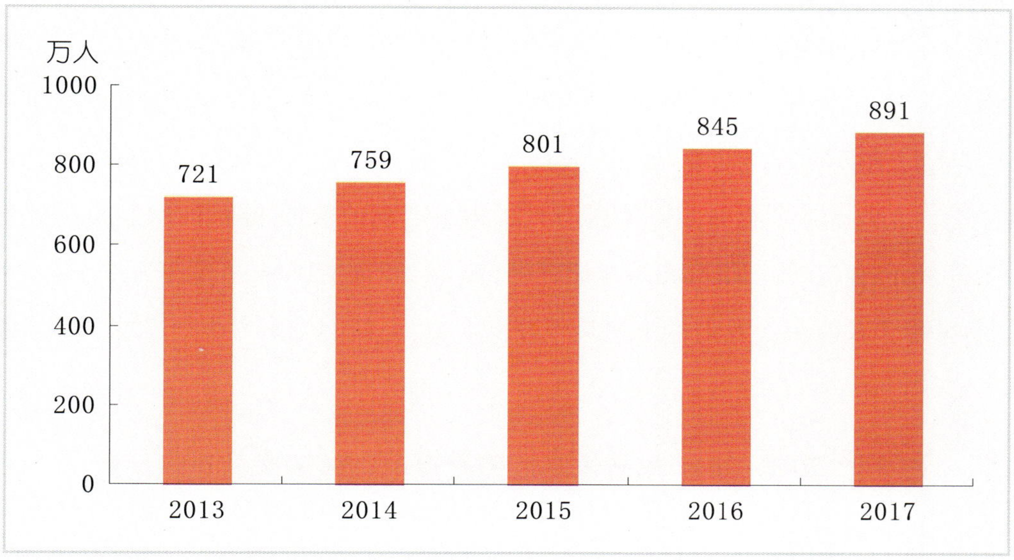

年末全国共有各类提供住宿的社会服务机构 3.2 万个，其中养老服务机构 2.9 万个，儿童服务机构 656 个。社会服务床位[66]749.5 万张，其中养老服务床位 714.2 万张，儿童服务床位 9.6 万张。年末共有社区服务中心 2.5 万个，社区服务站 13.9 万个。

十二、资源、环境和安全生产

全年全国国有建设用地供应总量[67]60 万公顷，比上年增长 16.4%。其中，工矿仓储用地 12 万公顷，增长 1.6%；房地产用地[68]11.5 万公顷，增长 7.2%；基础设施等用地 36.5 万公顷，增长 26.1%。

全年水资源总量 28675 亿立方米。全年平均降水量 640 毫米。年末全国监测的 604 座大型水库蓄水总量 3518 亿立方米，比上年末蓄水量有所增加。全年总用水量 6090 亿立方米，比上年增长 0.8%。其中，生活用水增长 2.8%，工业用水增长 0.2%，农业用水增长 0.6%，生态补水增长 1.7%。万元国内生产总值用水量[69]78 立方米，比上年下降 5.6%。万元工业增加值用水量 49 立方米，下降 5.9%。人均用水量 439 立方米，比上年增长 0.3%。

[64] 总诊疗人次指所有诊疗工作的总人次数，包括门诊、急诊、出诊、预约诊疗、单项健康检查、健康咨询指导（不含健康讲座）人次。

[65] 出院人数指报告期内所有住院后出院的人数，包括医嘱离院、医嘱转其他医疗机构、非医嘱离院、死亡及其他人数，不含家庭病床撤床人数。

[66] 社会服务床位数除收养性机构外，还包括救助类机构、社区类机构以及军休所、军供站等机构的床位。

[67] 国有建设用地供应总量是指报告期内市、县人民政府根据年度土地供应计划依法以出让、划拨、租赁等方式将土地使用权提供给单位或个人使用的国有建设用地总量。

[68] 房地产用地是指商服用地和住宅用地的总和。

[69] 万元国内生产总值用水量、万元工业增加值用水量和万元国内生产总值能耗按 2015 年价格计算。

全年完成造林面积736万公顷，其中人工造林面积390万公顷，占全部造林面积的53.0%。森林抚育面积830万公顷。截至年底，自然保护区达到2750个，其中国家级自然保护区463个。新增水土流失治理面积5.6万平方公里。

初步核算，全年能源消费总量44.9亿吨标准煤，比上年增长2.9%。煤炭消费量增长0.4%，原油消费量增长5.2%，天然气消费量增长14.8%，电力消费量增长6.6%。煤炭消费量占能源消费总量的60.4%，比上年下降1.6个百分点；天然气、水电、核电、风电等清洁能源消费量占能源消费总量的20.8%，上升1.3个百分点。全国万元国内生产总值能耗下降3.7%。重点耗能工业企业单位烧碱综合能耗下降0.3%，吨水泥综合能耗下降0.1%，吨钢综合能耗下降0.9%，吨粗铜综合能耗下降4.8%，每千瓦时火力发电标准煤耗下降0.8%。全国万元国内生产总值二氧化碳排放下降5.1%。

图24 2013—2017年清洁能源消费量占能源消费总量的比重

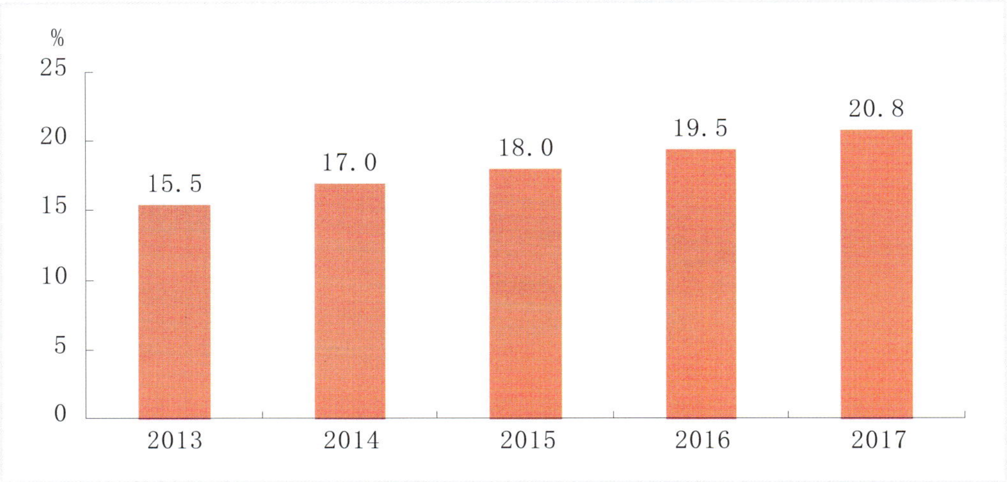

近岸海域417个海水水质监测点中，达到国家一、二类海水水质标准的监测点占67.8%，三类海水占10.1%，四类、劣四类海水占22.1%。

在监测的338个地级及以上城市中，城市空气质量达标的城市占29.3%，未达标的城市占70.7%。细颗粒物（$PM_{2.5}$）未达标城市（基于2015年$PM_{2.5}$年平均浓度未达标的262个城市）年平均浓度48微克/立方米，比上年下降5.9%。

在监测的323个城市中，城市区域声环境质量好的城市占5.9%，较好的占65.0%，一般的占27.9%，较差的占0.9%，差的占0.3%。

全年平均气温为10.39℃，比上年上升0.03℃。共有8个台风登陆。

全年农作物受灾面积1848万公顷，其中绝收183万公顷。全年因洪涝和地质灾害造成直接经济损失 1910 亿元，因旱灾造成直接经济损失 375 亿元，因低温冷冻和雪灾造成直接经济损失 19 亿元，因海洋灾害造成直接经济损失 58 亿元。全年大陆地区共发生 5.0 级以上地震 13 次，成灾 11 次，造成直接经济损失 148 亿元。全年共发生森林火灾 3223 起，森林火灾受害森林面积 2.5 万公顷。

全年各类生产安全事故共死亡 37852 人。工矿商贸企业就业人员 10 万人生产安全事故死亡人数 1.639 人，比上年下降 3.7%；道路交通事故万车死亡人数 2.06 人，下降 3.7%；煤矿百万吨死亡人数 0.106 人，下降 32.1%。

资料来源：

本公报中户籍人口城镇化率、民用汽车、交通事故数据来自公安部；城镇新增就业、登记失业率、社会保障、技工学校数据来自人力资源社会保障部；外汇储备、汇率数据来自外汇局；财政数据来自财政部；制造业产品质量合格率、质量检验、国家标准制定修订等数据来自质检总局；水产品产量数据来自农业部；木材产量、林业、森林火灾数据来自林业局；灌溉面积、水资源、水土流失治理数据来自水利部；发电装机容量、新增 220 千伏及以上变电设备数据来自中电联；新建铁路投产里程、增新建铁路复线投产里程、电气化铁路投产里程、铁路运输数据来自铁路总公司；新改建公路里程、港口万吨级码头泊位新增通过能力、公路运输、水运、港口货物吞吐量数据来自交通运输部；新增民用运输机场、民航数据来自民航局；新增光缆线路长度、电信业务总量、电话交换机容量、电话用户、宽带用户、移动互联网接入流量、上网人数、互联网普及率、软件业务收入等数据来自工业和信息化部；棚户区住房改造、公租房、农村地区建档立卡贫困户危房改造数据来自住房城乡建设部；货物进出口数据来自海关总署；服务进出口、外商直接投资、对外直接投资、对外承包工程、对外劳务合作等数据来自商务部；管道数据来自中石油、中石化、中海油；邮政业务数据来自邮政局；农村地区互联网普及率数据来自中国互联网络信息中心；旅游数据来自旅游局、公安部；货币金融、公司信用类债券数据来自人民银行；上市公司数据来自证监会；保险业数据来自保监会；城乡低保、农村特困人员救助供养、社会服务、农作物受灾面积、洪涝地质灾害造成直接经济损失、旱灾造成直接经济损失、低温冷冻和雪灾造成直接经济损失来自民政部；教育数据来自教育部；重点研发计划、科技重大专项、国家重点实验室、科技成果转化引导基金、技术合同等数据来自科技部；自然科学基金项目数据来自自然基金委；国家工程研究中心、国家工程实验室、企业技术中心、万元国内生产总值二氧化碳排放等数据来自发展改革委；专利数据来自知识产权局；宇航发射数据来自国防科工局；艺术表演团体、博物馆、公共图书馆、文化馆数据来自文化部；广播电视、电影、报纸、期刊、图书数据来自新闻出版广电总局；档案数据来自档案局；体育数据来自体育总局；残疾人运动员数据来自中国残联；卫生数据来自卫生计生委；国有建设用地供应数据来自国土资源部；自然保护区、环境监测数据来自环境保护部；平均气温、登陆台风数据来自气象局；海洋灾害造成直接经济损失数据来自海洋局；地震次数、地震灾害直接经济损失数据来自地震局；安全生产数据来自安全监管总局；其他数据均来自国家统计局。

STATISTICAL COMMUNIQUÉ OF THE PEOPLE'S REPUBLIC OF CHINA ON THE 2017 NATIONAL ECONOMIC AND SOCIAL DEVELOPMENT[1]

National Bureau of Statistics of China
February 28, 2018

In 2017, under the leadership of the Central Committee of the Communist Party of China with Comrade Xi Jinping as the core, all regions and departments have steadily strengthened their consciousness of the need to maintain political integrity, think in big-picture terms, uphold the leadership core and keep in alignment, implemented the spirit of the 18th National Congress of the Communist Party of China and the third, forth, fifth, sixth and seventh plenary sessions of the 18th Central Committee of the Communist Party of China, studied and carried out the spirit of the 19th National Congress of the Communist Party of China and taken Xi Jinping Thought on Socialism with Chinese Characteristics for a New Era as the guideline. Following the arrangements of the Central Economic Working Conference and the Report on the Work of the Government, all regions and departments have adhered to the general working guideline of making progress while maintaining stability, stuck to the new development philosophy, taken the improvement of the

1. All figures in this Communiqué are preliminary statistics. Statistics in this Communiqué do not include Hong Kong SAR, Macao SAR and Taiwan Province. Due to the rounding-off reasons, the subentries may not add up to the aggregate totals.

quality and efficacy of development as the core, promoted balanced economic, political, cultural, social and ecological progress, coordinated the implementation of the four-pronged comprehensive strategy, focused on the supply-side structural reform and coordinated the efforts in stabilizing growth, stimulating reform, adjusting structure, benefiting people's livelihood and fending off risks. As a result, the national economy has maintained the momentum of stable and sound development and exceeded the expectation and the economy and society are moving forward steadily and healthily.

I. General Outlook

According to preliminary accounting, the gross domestic product (GDP)[2] in 2017 was 82,712.2 billion yuan, up by 6.9 percent over the previous year. Of this total, the value added of the primary industry was 6,546.8 billion yuan, up by 3.9 percent, that of the secondary industry was 33,462.3 billion yuan, up by 6.1 percent and that of the tertiary industry was 42,703.2 billion yuan, up by 8.0 percent. The value added of the primary industry accounted for 7.9 percent of the GDP; that of the secondary industry accounted for 40.5 percent; and that of the tertiary industry accounted for 51.6 percent. The contribution of the final consumption expenditure to GDP accounted for 58.8 percent, that of the gross capital formation 32.1 percent and that of the net exports of goods and services 9.1 percent. The per capita GDP in 2017 was 59,660 yuan, up by 6.3 percent compared with the previous year. The gross national income[3] in 2017 was 82,501.6 billion yuan, up by 7.0 percent over the previous year.

Figure 1 : Gross Domestic Product and the Growth Rates 2013-2017

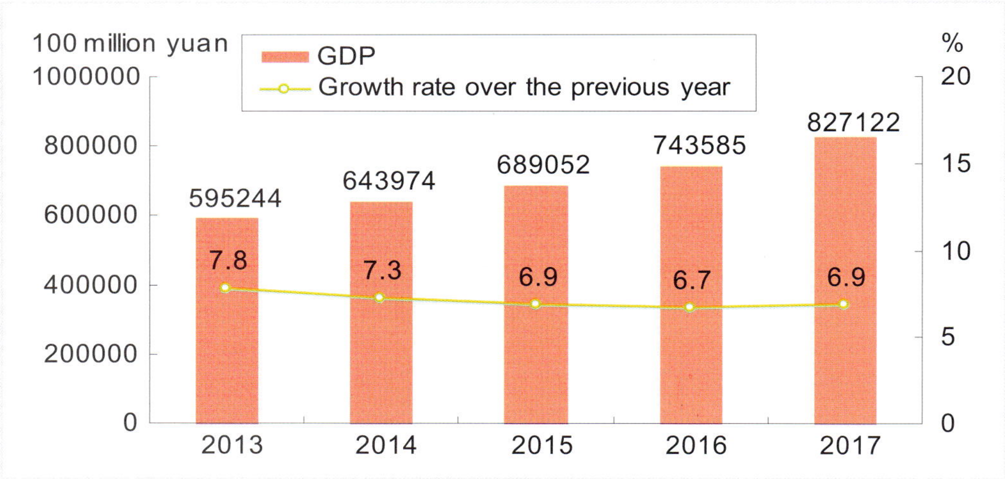

2. Gross domestic product (GDP), value added and per capita GDP as quoted in this Communiqué are calculated at current prices whereas their growth rates are at constant prices.

3. Gross national income, also known as gross national product, refers to the total primary distribution of the income created by all the resident units of a country (or a region) during a certain period of time. It equals to gross domestic product plus the net primary distribution of income from abroad.

Figure 2 : Shares of the Three Industries' Value Added of GDP 2013-2017

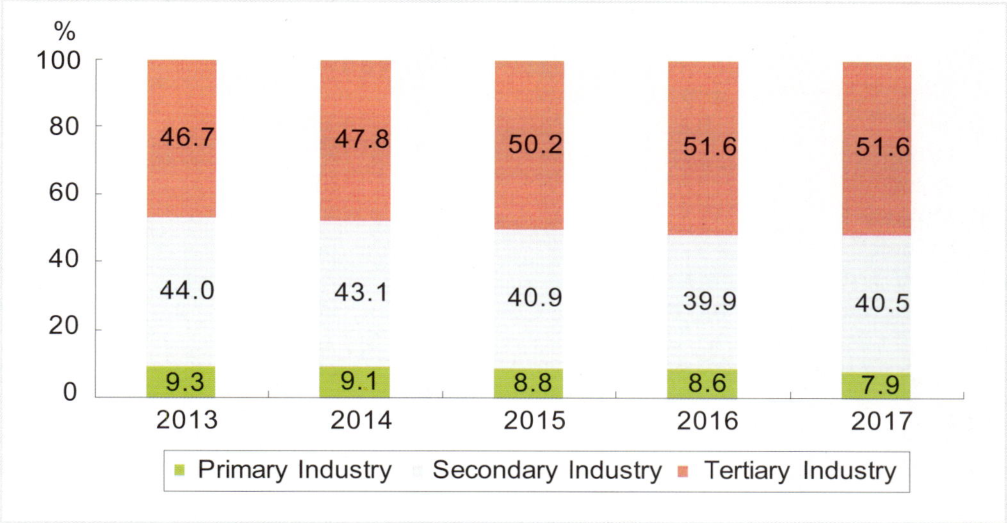

By the end of 2017, the total number of Chinese population at the mainland reached 1,390.08 million, an increase of 7.37 million over that at the end of 2016. Of this total, urban permanent residents numbered 813.47 million, accounting for 58.52 percent of the total population (the urbanization rate of permanent residents), and 1.17 percentage points higher than that at the end of last year. The urbanization rate of population with household registration was 42.35 percent, 1.15 percentage points higher than that at the end of 2016. The year 2017 saw 17.23 million births, a crude birth rate of 12.43 per thousand, and 9.86 million deaths, a crude death rate of 7.11 per thousand. The natural growth rate was 5.32 per thousand. The number of population who live in places other than their household registration areas[4] reached 291 million, of which 244 million were floating population[5].

4. Population who live in places other than their household registration areas refers to those who reside in areas other than their household registration and have been away from there for over 6 months.

5. Floating population refers to the population who live in places other than their household registration excluding those with current residences different from the places of their household registration but still in the same city. Population who live in places other than their household registration but still in the same city refers to those whose current residences are different from the registered towns or streets in the same district or in different districts but still in the same municipality or prefecture-level city.

Table 1 : Population and Its Composition by the End of 2017

Item	Population (Year-end figure) (10,000 persons)	Proportion (%)
National Total	**139008**	**100.0**
Of which: Urban	81347	58.52
Rural	57661	41.48
Of which: Male	71137	51.2
Female	67871	48.8
Of which: Aged 0-15 (under the age of 16) [6]	24719	17.8
Aged 16-59 (under the age of 60)	90199	64.9
Aged 60 and above	24090	17.3
Of which: Aged 65 and above	15831	11.4

At the end of 2017, the number of employed people in China was 776.40 million, and that in urban areas was 424.62 million. The newly increased employed people in urban areas numbered 13.51 million, 0.37 million more than last year. The registered urban unemployment rate was 3.90 percent at the year end, 0.12 percentage point lower than the end of last year. The total number of migrant workers[7] in 2017 was 286.52 million, up by 1.7 percent over that of 2016. Specifically, the number of migrant workers who left their hometowns and worked in other places was 171.85 million, increased by 1.5 percent, and those who worked in their own localities reached 114.67 million, up by 2.0 percent.

Figure 3 : Newly Increased Employed People in Urban Areas 2013-2017

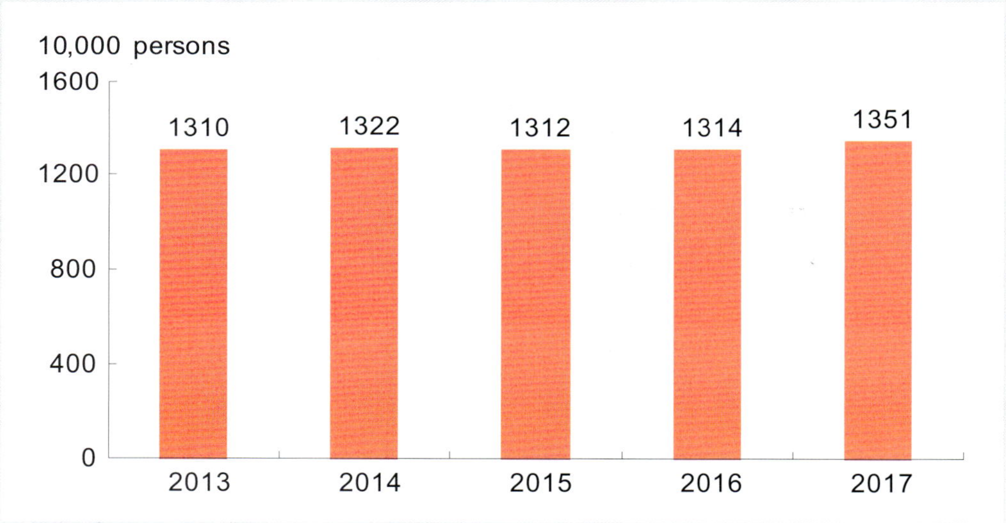

6. By the end of 2017, the population aged 0 to 14 (under the age of 15) was 233.48 million and that aged 15 to 59 (under the age of 60) was 915.70 million.

7. The number of migrant workers includes those who are employed outside their villages and towns for more than six months in the year and those who do non-agricultural work in their villages and towns for more than six months in the year.

The consumer prices in 2017 went up by 1.6 percent over the previous year. The producer prices went up by 6.3 percent and the purchasing prices for manufactured goods up by 8.1 percent. The prices for investment in fixed assets increased by 5.8 percent. The producer prices for farm products[8] decreased by 3.5 percent.

Figure 4 : Monthly Changes of Consumer Prices in 2017

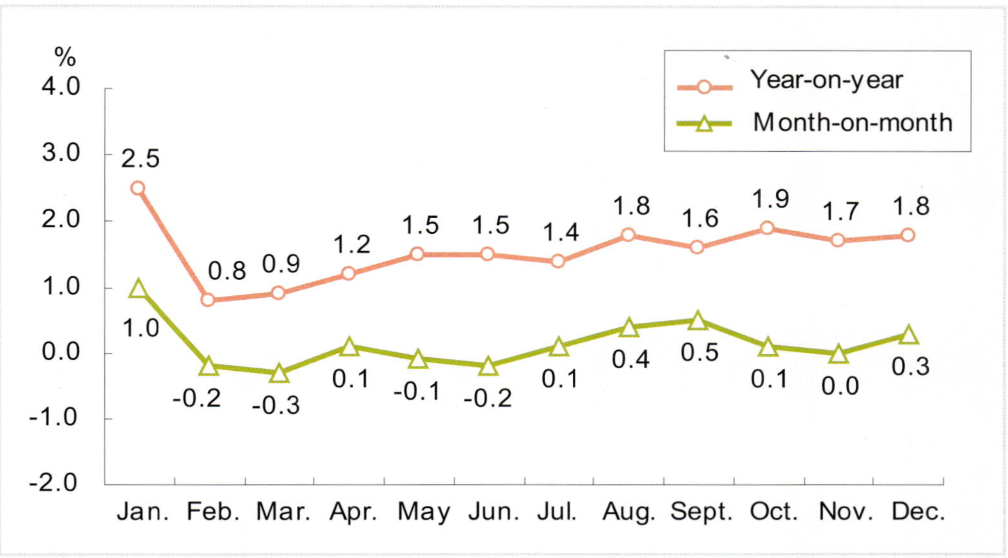

Table 2: Changes of Consumer Prices in 2017

Unit: %

Item	National Average	Urban	Rural
General level of consumer prices	**1.6**	**1.7**	**1.3**
Of which: Food, tobacco and liquor	-0.4	-0.2	-1.1
Clothing	1.3	1.2	1.3
Residence[9]	2.6	2.5	2.7
Household facilities, articles and services	1.1	1.0	1.2
Transportation and telecommunication	1.1	1.0	1.4
Education, culture and recreation	2.4	2.4	2.3
Health care and medical services	6.0	6.8	4.2
Miscellaneous goods and services	2.4	2.5	2.4

8. The producer prices for farm products refer to the prices of farm products sold directly by producers.
9. The prices for residence include prices for rent, maintenance and management, water, electricity and fuel etc.

In December, out of the 70 large-and-medium-sized cities, 61 cities showed a year-on-year rise in sales prices of new commercial residential buildings, which was 5 less than that in January, and 9 cities experienced a decline, which was 5 more than that in January.

Figure 5 : Year-on-year Changes of Cities Showing Rise and Decline in Prices of New Commercial Residential Buildings in 2017

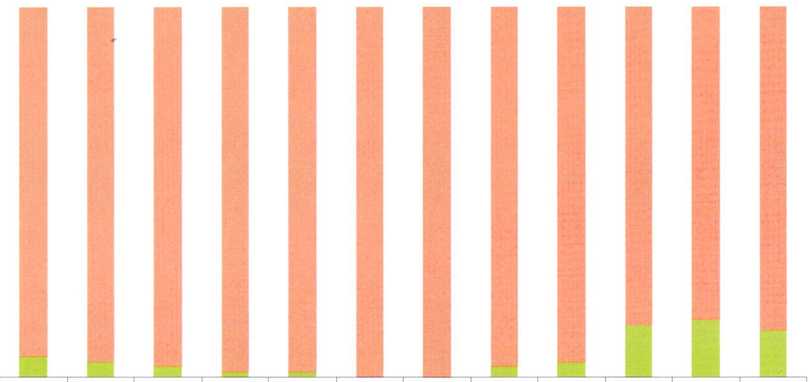

	Jan.	Feb.	Mar.	Apr.	May	Jun.	Jul.	Aug.	Sept.	Oct.	Nov.	Dec.
Rise	66	67	68	69	69	70	70	68	67	60	59	61
Decline	4	3	2	1	1	0	0	2	3	10	11	9

At the end of 2017, China's foreign exchange reserves reached 3,139.9 billion US dollars, an increase of 129.4 billion US dollars as compared with that at the end of 2016. The average exchange rate of the year was 6.7518 RMB to 1 USD dollar, depreciated by 1.6 percent over that of 2016.

Figure 6 : Year-end China's Foreign Exchange Reserves 2013-2017

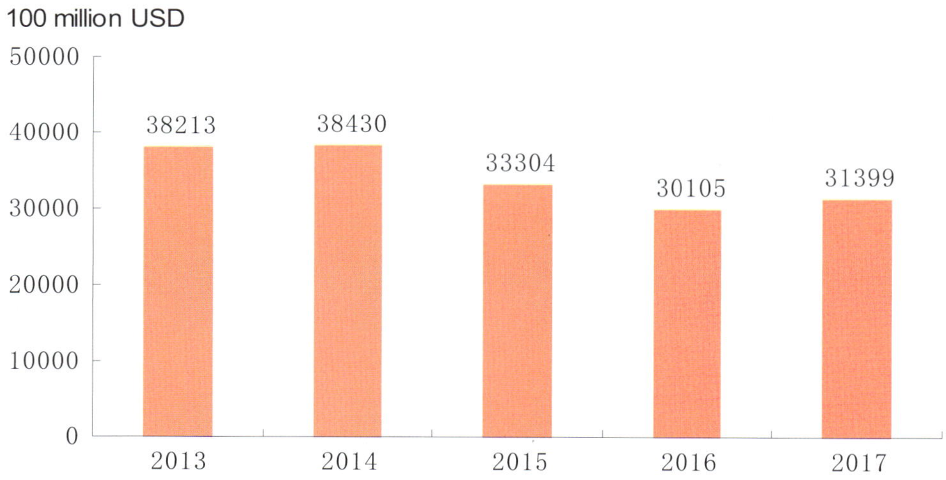

The supply-side structural reform was pushed forward solidly. In 2017, the national industrial capacity utilization rate[10] reached 77.0 percent, 3.7 percentage points higher than last year. Specifically, the capacity utilization rate for mining and washing of coal was 68.2 percent, 8.7 percentage points higher than last year and that for smelting and pressing of ferrous metals was 75.8 percent, 4.1 percentage points higher. At the end of 2017, the floor space of commercial buildings for sale was 589.23 million square meters, 106.16 million square meters less than that at the end of 2016. Specifically, the floor space of the commercial residential buildings for sale was 301.63 million square meters, 100.94 million square meters less. At the end of 2017, the asset-liability ratio of the industrial enterprises above the designated size was 55.5 percent, 0.6 percentage point less than that at the end of 2016. In 2017, the cost for per-hundred-yuan turnover of principal activities of the industrial enterprises above the designated size was 84.92 yuan, 0.25 yuan less compared with last year; the expense for per-hundred-yuan turnover of principal activities was 7.77 yuan, a decrease of 0.2 yuan. In 2017, the fixed assets investment in ecological protection and treatment of environmental pollution, public facilities management and agriculture (excluding by rural households) went up by 23.9 percent, 21.8 percent and 16.4 percent compared with last year.

The growth of new driving forces, new industries and new forms of businesses accelerated. In 2017, the value added of the industrial strategic emerging industries[11] above the designated size grew by 11.0 percent compared with last year. The value added of the high technology manufacturing industry[12] was up by 13.4 percent over the previous year, accounting for 12.7 percent of that of the industrial enterprises above the designated size. The value added for manufacture of equipment[13] was up by 11.3 percent, accounting for 32.7 percent of that of industrial enterprises above the designated size. In 2017, the production of new energy vehicles reached 0.69 million, up by 51.2 percent compared with last year; that of smart TV sets 96.66 million, up by 3.8 percent; that of industrial robots 0.13 million, up by 81.0 percent; that of civilian drones 2.90

10. Capacity utilization rate refers to the ratio of the actual production to the production capacity (in terms of value). Actual production refers to the total industrial output value during the enterprise's reporting period. Production capacity refers to the production which can be realized and sustained for a long term under the condition of the supply of labor force, materials, fuel and transportation guaranteed and the production equipment in proper operation.

11. Industrial strategic emerging industries refer to the related industrial sectors of energy-saving and environmental protection, information technology of new generation, biotech, manufacture of high-end equipment, new energy, new materials, and new energy cars.

12. High technology manufacturing industry includes manufacture of medicine, manufacture of aerospace vehicle and equipment, manufacture of electronic and communication equipment, manufacture of computers and office equipment, manufacture of medical equipment, manufacture of measuring instrument and equipment and manufacture of optical and photographic equipment.

13. Manufacture of equipment includes manufacture of metal products, general purpose equipment, special purpose equipment, automobiles, railway, ship, aerospace and other transport equipment, electrical machinery and apparatus, computers, communication and other electric equipment and measuring instrument and machinery.

million, up by 67.0 percent. Among the service enterprises above the designated size[14], the business revenue of the strategic emerging service industries[15] reached 4,123.5 billion yuan, up by 17.3 percent; the operating profit reached 744.6 billion yuan, up by 30.2 percent. In 2017, the investment in high technology industries[16] reached 4,291.2 billion yuan, an increase of 15.9 percent over last year, accounting for 6.8 percent of the investment in fixed assets (excluding by rural households); the investment in industrial technological transformation[17] was 10,591.2 billion yuan, up by 16.3 percent, accounting for 16.8 percent of the investment in fixed assets (excluding by rural households). The online retail sales[18] were 7,175.1 billion yuan in 2017, an increase of 32.2 percent compared with the previous year. The online retail sales of commodities were 5,480.6 billion yuan, an increase of 28.0 percent, accounting for 15.0 percent of the total retail sales of consumer goods. Among online retail sales of commodities, the sales of food increased by 28.6 percent, clothing by 20.3 percent and daily necessities by 30.8 percent. By the end of 2016, 25.1 percent of villages in China had set up e-commerce distribution sites.

The quality and efficacy of development improved. The general public budget revenue reached 17,256.7 billion yuan in 2017, up by 7.4 percent over the previous year[19]. Of this total, the taxes collected in 2017 reached 14,436.0 billion yuan, an increase of 1,399.9 billion yuan or up by 10.7 percent. The profits made by the industrial enterprises above the designated size in 2017 were 7,518.7 billion yuan, an increase of 21.0 percent over the previous year. By ownership, the profits of state-holding enterprises were 1,665.1

14. Service enterprises above the designated size refer to legal entities of transport, storage and post, information transmission, software and information technology services, real estate (excluding real estate development and operation), leasing and business services, scientific research and technical services, water conservancy, environment and public facilities management, education, health and social work with annual business revenue of 10 million yuan and above or with 50 employees and above at the end of the year; legal entities of services to households, repair and other services and culture, sports and entertainment with annual business revenue of 5 million and above or with 50 employees and above at the end of the year.

15. Strategic emerging service industries refer to the related service sectors of energy-saving and environmental protection, information technology of new generation, biotech, manufacture of high-end equipment, new energy, new materials, and new energy cars.

16. Investment in high technology industries refers to investment in six high technology manufacturing industries, including the manufacture of medicine and manufacture of aerospace vehicle and equipment, and nine high technology service industries, including information service and e-commerce service.

17. Investment in industrial technological transformation refers to the investment in the improvement of the existing equipments, technologies and production services through new technologies, crafts, equipments and materials so as to achieve intensive development.

18. Online retail sales refer to the retail sales of goods and services realized through internet trading platforms (online platforms mainly in trading physical commodities, including self-built websites and third-party platforms). The sales of services of online retail and a few other goods for production operation and resale are not covered by the total retail sales of consumer goods.

19. To facilitate the coordinated use of financial funds, starting from January 1, 2017, 3 items under the government budget funds including land use fee for additional construction land, fund for South-to-North Water Diversion Project and special payment from tobacco enterprises were reallocated under the general public budget. To this end, the base of the year 2016 has taken the effect of the reallocation of the 3 items into consideration, based on which the year-on-year changes both in volume and in growth rate were calculated.

billion yuan, up by 45.1 percent; those of collective enterprises 40.0 billion yuan, down by 8.5 percent; those of share-holding enterprises 5,240.4 billion yuan, up by 23.5 percent; those of the enterprises by foreign investors and investors from Hong Kong, Macao and Taiwan 1,875.3 billion yuan, up by 15.8 percent; and those of private enterprises 2,375.3 billion yuan, up by 11.7 percent. In terms of different sectors, the profit of mining was 458.7 billion yuan, an increase of 2.6 times compared with last year; those of manufacturing 6,651.1 billion yuan, up by 18.2 percent; those of the production and supply of electricity, heat power, gas and water 408.9 billion yuan, down by 10.7 percent. In 2017, the operating profit of service enterprises above the designated size reached 2,364.5 billion yuan, an increase of 24.5 percent. The overall labor productivity[20] was 101,231 yuan per person in 2017, an increase of 6.7 percent compared with that in 2016. In 2017, the qualification rate of manufactured products[21] reached 93.71 percent.

Figure 7 : General Public Budget Revenue 2013-2017

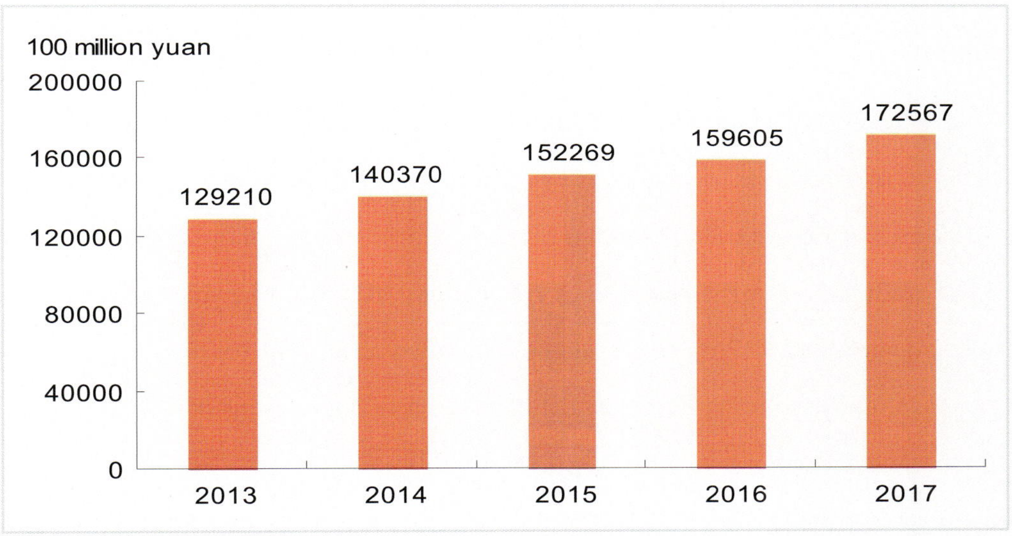

Note: Data for general public budget revenue from 2013 to 2016 as shown in the figure were final accounts, and that of 2017 was executive accounts.

20. The overall labor productivity refers to the ratio between the GDP (at 2015 constant price) and the total number of persons employed.

21. Qualification rate of manufactured products is the ratio of the samples that have passed the sampling quality test, the process of which follows certain methods, procedure and standard, to the total amount of the sampled products. The survey samples cover 29 sectors of the manufacturing industry.

Figure 8 : Overall Labor Productivity 2013-2017

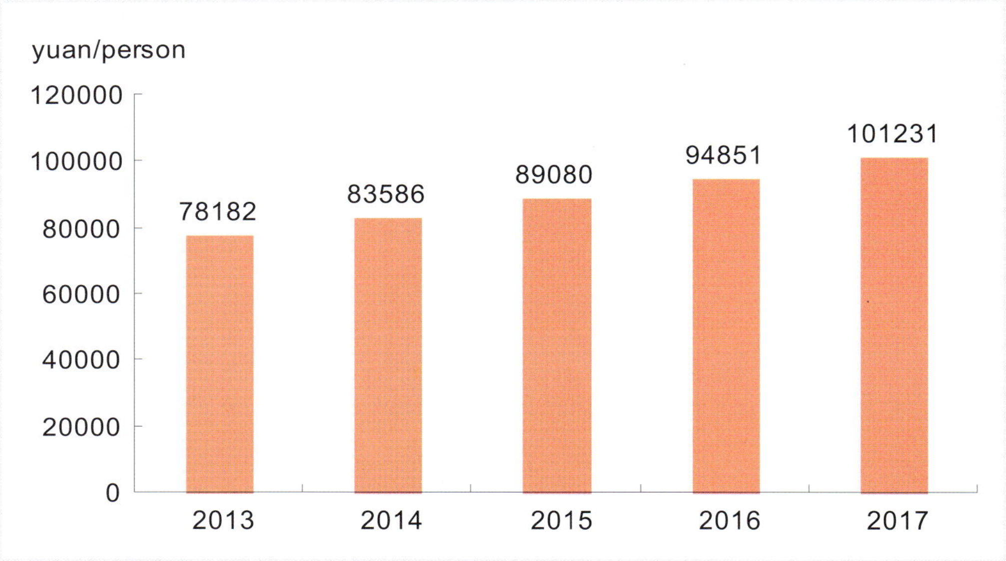

II. Agriculture

In 2017, the sown area of grain was 112.22 million hectares, a drop of 0.81 million hectares compared with that in 2016. Of this total, the sown area of wheat was 23.99 million hectares, a decrease of 0.2 million hectares; the sown area of rice was 30.18 million hectares, a decrease of 2 thousand hectares; the sown area of corn was 35.45 million hectares, a decrease of 1.32 million hectares. The sown area of cotton was 3.23 million hectares, a decrease of 0.12 million hectares. The sown area of oil-bearing crops was 14.20 million hectares, an increase of 70 thousand hectares; the sown area of sugar crops was 1.68 million hectares, a decrease of 10 thousand hectares.

The total output of grain in 2017 was 617.91 million tons, an increase of 1.66 million tons or up by 0.3 percent over the previous year. Of this total, the output of summer crops was 140.31 million tons, up by 0.8 percent, and that of the early rice was 31.74 million tons, down by 3.2 percent over the previous year. The output of autumn grain was 445.85 million tons, up by 0.4 percent. The output of cereal was 564.55 million tons, a decrease of 0.1 percent, among which the output of rice was 208.56 million tons, up by 0.7 percent; that of wheat was 129.77 million tons, up by 0.7 percent; and that of corn was 215.89 million tons, down by 1.7 percent.

Figure 9 : Output of Grain 2013-2017

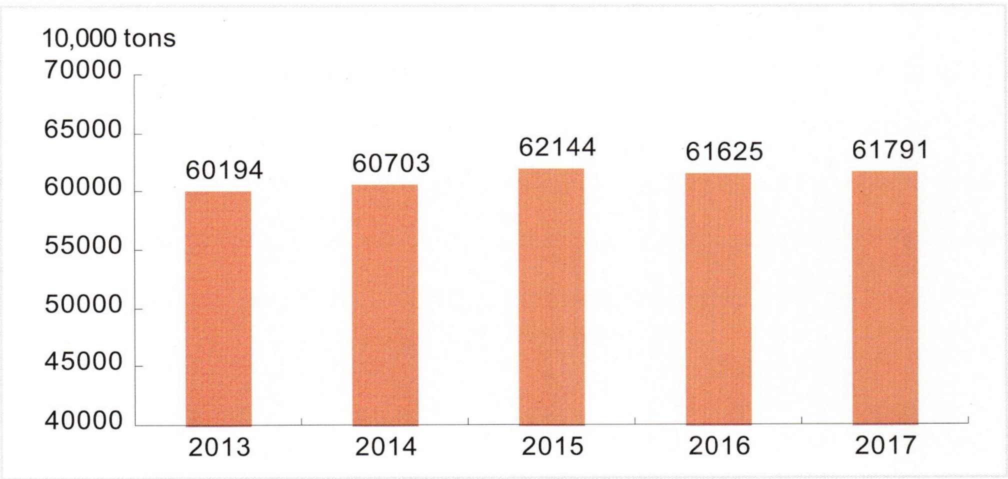

In 2017, the output of cotton was 5.49 million tons, an increase of 3.5 percent over the previous year, that of oil-bearing crops was 37.32 million tons, an increase of 2.8 percent, that of sugar crops was 125.56 million tons, an increase of 1.7 percent, and that of tea was 2.55 million tons, up by 6.0 percent.

The total output of pork, beef, mutton and poultry in 2017 reached 84.31 million tons, up by 0.8 percent over the previous year. Of this total, the output of pork was 53.40 million tons, up by 0.8 percent; that of beef was 7.26 million tons, up by 1.3 percent; that of mutton was 4.68 million tons, an increase of 1.8 percent; and that of poultry was 18.97 million tons, an increase of 0.5 percent. The total output of eggs was 30.70 million tons, down by 0.8 percent. The production of milk was 35.45 million tons, down by 1.6 percent. At the end of the year, 433.25 million pigs were registered in the total stocks, down by 0.4 percent, and 688.61 million pigs were slaughtered, up by 0.5 percent.

The total output of aquatic products in 2017 was 69.38 million tons, up by 0.5 percent over the previous year. Of this total, the output of cultured aquatic products was 52.81 million tons, up by 2.7 percent; and that of fished aquatic products was 16.56 million tons, down by 5.8 percent over the previous year.

The total production of timber for the year 2017 reached 76.82 million cubic meters, a decrease of 1.2 percent compared with the previous year.

Over 1.09 million hectares of farmland were newly equipped with effective irrigation systems and another 1.44 million hectares of farmland was newly equipped with water-saving irrigation systems.

III. Industry and Construction

In 2017, the total value added of the industrial sector was 27,999.7 billion yuan, up by 6.4 percent over the previous year. The value added of industrial enterprises above the designated size increased by 6.6

percent. Of the industrial enterprises above the designated size, in terms of ownership, the value added of the state-holding enterprises grew by 6.5 percent, that of the collective enterprises up by 0.6 percent, that of the share-holding enterprises up by 6.6 percent, that of the enterprises by foreign investors and investors from Hong Kong, Macao and Taiwan up by 6.9 percent and that of private enterprises up by 5.9 percent. In terms of sectors, the value added of the mining industry was down by 1.5 percent, that of manufacturing up by 7.2 percent and that of production and supply of electricity, heat power, gas and water up by 8.1 percent.

Figure 10 : Value Added and Its Growth Rates of Industrial Enterprises 2013-2017

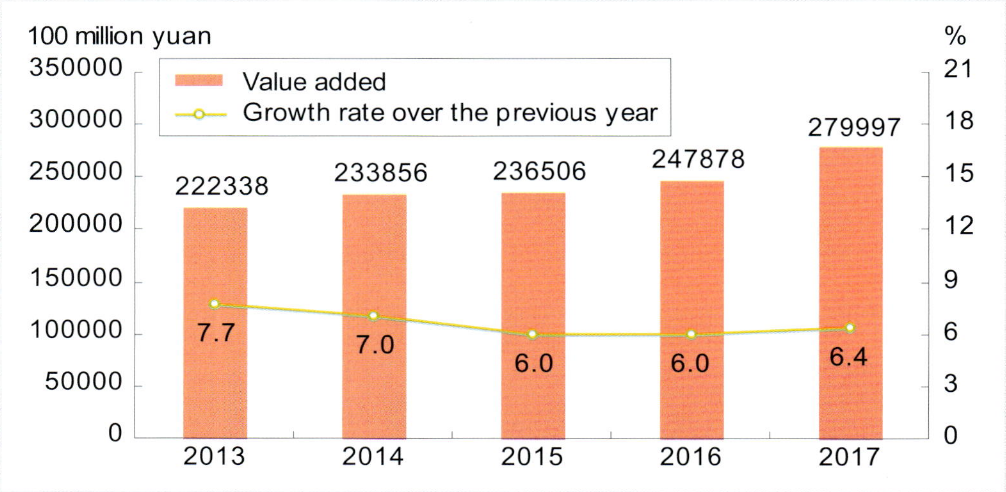

In 2017, of the industrial enterprises above the designated size, the value added for processing of food from agricultural and sideline products was up by 6.8 percent over the previous year; for textile industry up by 4.0 percent; for manufacture of raw chemical materials and chemical products up by 3.8 percent; for manufacture of non-metallic mineral products up by 3.7 percent; for smelting and pressing of ferrous metals up by 0.3 percent; for manufacture of general purpose machinery up by 10.5 percent; for manufacture of special purpose machinery up by 11.8 percent; for manufacture of automobiles up by 12.2 percent; for manufacture of electrical machinery and apparatus up by 10.6 percent; for manufacture of computers, communication equipment and other electronic equipment up by 13.8 percent; for production and supply of electricity and heat power up by 7.8 percent. The growth of the value added for the six major high energy consuming industries[22] was 3.0 percent, accounting for 29.7 percent of the value added of industrial enterprises above the designated size.

22. The six major high energy consuming industries consist of processing of petroleum, coking and processing of nuclear fuel, manufacture of raw chemical materials and chemical products, manufacture of non-metallic mineral products, smelting and pressing of ferrous metals, smelting and pressing of non-ferrous metals and production and supply of electricity and heat power.

Table 3: Output of Major Industrial Products and Their Growth Rates in 2017

Product	Unit	Output	Increase over 2016 (%)
Yarn	10000 tons	4050.0	8.5
Cloth	100 million meters	868.1	-4.3
Chemical fiber	10000 tons	4919.6	0.7
Refined sugar (final product)	10000 tons	1470.6	1.9
Cigarettes	100 million	23448.3	-1.6
Color TV sets	10000	15932.6	1.0
Of which: LCD TV sets	10000	15755.9	0.3
Household refrigerators	10000	8548.4	0.8
Air conditioners	10000	17861.5	24.5
Primary energy output	100 million tons of standard coal equivalent	35.9	3.6
Coal	100 million tons	35.2	3.3
Crude petroleum oil	10000 tons	19150.6	-4.1
Natural gas	100 million cubic meters	1480.3	8.2
Electricity	100 million kilowatt-hours	64951.4	5.9
Of which: Thermal power[23]	100 million kilowatt-hours	46627.4	5.1
Hydropower	100 million kilowatt-hours	11898.4	0.5
Nuclear-power	100 million kilowatt-hours	2480.7	16.3
Crude steel	10000 tons	83172.8	3.0
Rolled steel[24]	10000 tons	104958.8	0.1
Ten kinds of nonferrous metals	10000 tons	5501.0	2.9
Of which: Refined copper (copper)	10000 tons	897.0	6.3
Aluminum electrolyze	10000 tons	3329.0	2.0
Cement	100 million tons	23.4	-3.1
Sulfuric acid (100%)	10000 tons	9212.9	0.9
Caustic soda (100%)	10000 tons	3365.2	5.1
Ethylene	10000 tons	1821.8	2.3
Chemical fertilizers (100 percent equivalent)	10000 tons	6184.3	-6.7
Power generation equipment	10000 kilowatts	11830.4	-9.8
Motor vehicles	10000	2901.8	3.2
Of which: Basic passenger cars (cars)	10000	1194.5	-1.4
Sport utility vehicles (SUVs)	10000	1004.7	9.9
Large and medium tractors	10000	41.8	-32.4
Integrated circuits	100 million pieces	1564.6	18.7
Program-controlled switchboards	10000 lines	1240.8	-14.9
Mobile telephones[25]	10000	188982.4	2.2
Micro computer equipment	10000	30678.4	5.8

23. Thermal power refers to electricity generated by coal, oil, gas, residual heat, pressure and gas, waste incineration and biomass.
24. The data include 240.00 million tons of steel which has been reprocessed among enterprises.
25. The data of mobile telephones and the production of steel in 2016 were adjusted according to special surveys. The growth rates of production in 2017 were calculated on a comparable basis.

By the end of 2017, the installed power generation capacity was 1,777.03 million kilowatts, up by 7.6 percent over that at the end of 2016, among which[26] the installed thermal power generation capacity was 1,106.04 million kilowatts, up by 4.3 percent; the installed hydropower generation capacity was 341.19 million kilowatts, up by 2.7 percent; the installed nuclear power generation capacity was 35.82 million kilowatts, up by 6.5 percent. The installed grid-connected wind power generation capacity was 163.67 million kilowatts, up by 10.5 percent and the installed grid-connected solar power generation capacity was 130.25 million kilowatts, an increase of 68.7 percent.

In 2017, the value added of construction enterprises in China was 5,568.9 billion yuan, up by 4.3 percent over the previous year. The profits made by construction enterprises qualified for general contracts and specialized contracts reached 766.1 billion yuan, up by 9.7 percent, of which the profits made by state-holding enterprises were 231.3 billion yuan, up by 15.1 percent.

Figure 11 : Value Added and Its Growth Rates of Construction Industry 2013-2017

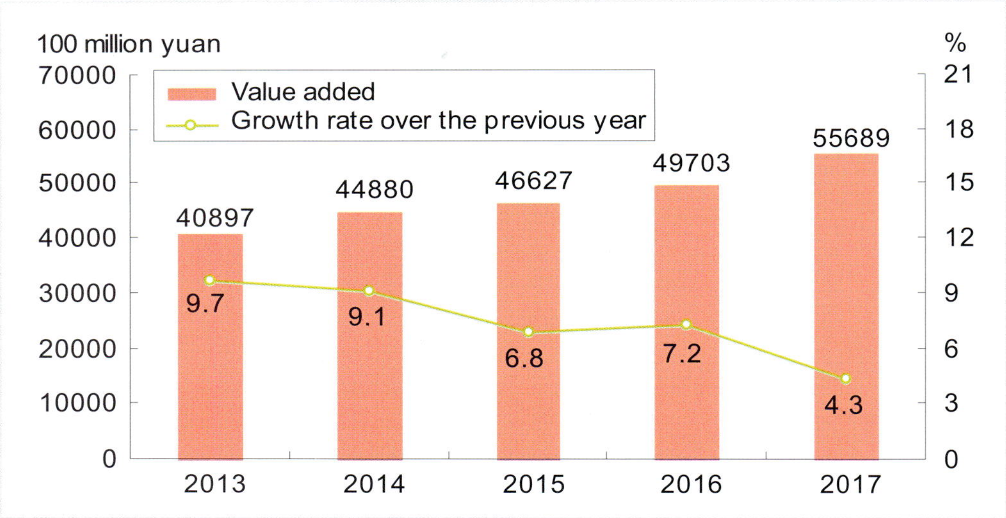

IV. Investment in Fixed Assets

The total investment in fixed assets of the country in 2017 was 64,123.8 billion yuan, up by 7.0 percent over the previous year[27]. Of the total investment, the investment in fixed assets (excluding by rural

26. Some installed power generation capacity was not listed (e.g. geothermal).
27. The base of the investment in fixed assets in 2016 was adjusted according to results of the third agricultural census and the growth rates in 2017 were calculated on a comparable basis.

households) was 63,168.4 billion yuan, up by 7.2 percent. By regions[28], the investment in eastern areas was 26,583.7 billion yuan, up by 8.3 percent over the previous year, in central areas 16,340.0 billion yuan, a growth of 6.9 percent, in western areas 16,657.1 billion yuan, a growth of 8.5 percent, and in northeastern areas 3,065.5 billion yuan, up by 2.8 percent.

In the investment in fixed assets (excluding by rural households), the investment in the primary industry was 2,089.2 billion yuan, up by 11.8 percent; that in the secondary industry was 23,575.1 billion yuan, up by 3.2 percent; and that in the tertiary industry was 37,504.0 billion yuan, up by 9.5 percent. The investment in infrastructure[29] was 14,000.5 billion yuan, up by 19.0 percent, accounting for 22.2 percent of the investment in fixed assets (excluding by rural households). The private investment[30] in fixed assets was 38,151.0 billion yuan, an increase of 6.0 percent, accounting for 60.4 percent of the total investment in fixed assets (excluding by rural households). The investment in the six major high energy consuming industries was 6,443.0 billion yuan, down by 1.8 percent, accounting for 10.2 percent of the investment in fixed assets (excluding by rural households).

Figure 12 : Shares of Investment in Fixed Assets of the Three Industries (Excluding by Rural Households) 2013-2017

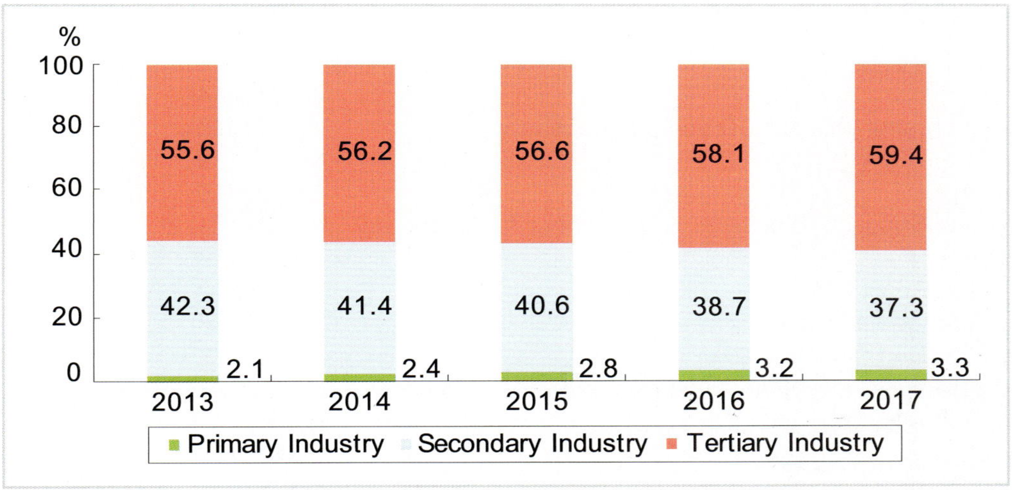

28. The national total investment in fixed assets (excluding by rural households) was larger than the aggregate of the subtotals of fixed assets investment in the eastern areas, central areas, western areas and northeastern areas due to the fact that some of the trans-regional investments are not covered by regional figures. The eastern areas include 10 provinces and municipalities: Beijing, Tianjin, Hebei, Shanghai, Jiangsu, Zhejiang, Fujian, Shandong, Guangdong and Hainan; the central areas cover 6 provinces: Shanxi, Anhui, Jiangxi, Henan, Hubei and Hunan; the western areas include 12 provinces, autonomous regions and municipalities: Inner Mongolia, Guangxi, Chongqing, Sichuan, Guizhou, Yunnan, Tibet, Shaanxi, Gansu, Qinghai, Ningxia and Xinjiang; the northeastern areas include 3 provinces: Liaoning, Jilin and Heilongjiang.

29. Investment in infrastructure refers to the investment in the construction or purchase of fundamental, public-serving projects and facilities for the social production and people's life, including transportation, postal service, telecommunication, radio, TV and satellite transmission, internet and related services, water conservancy, environment and public facilities management.

30. Private investment in fixed assets refers to investment in the construction or purchase of fixed assets by domestic collective, private and individual-owned enterprises or organizations or their holding enterprises (with absolute holding and relative holding enterprises).

Figure 13 : Investment in Fixed Assets by Sectors and Their Shares in 2017 (Excluding by Rural Households)

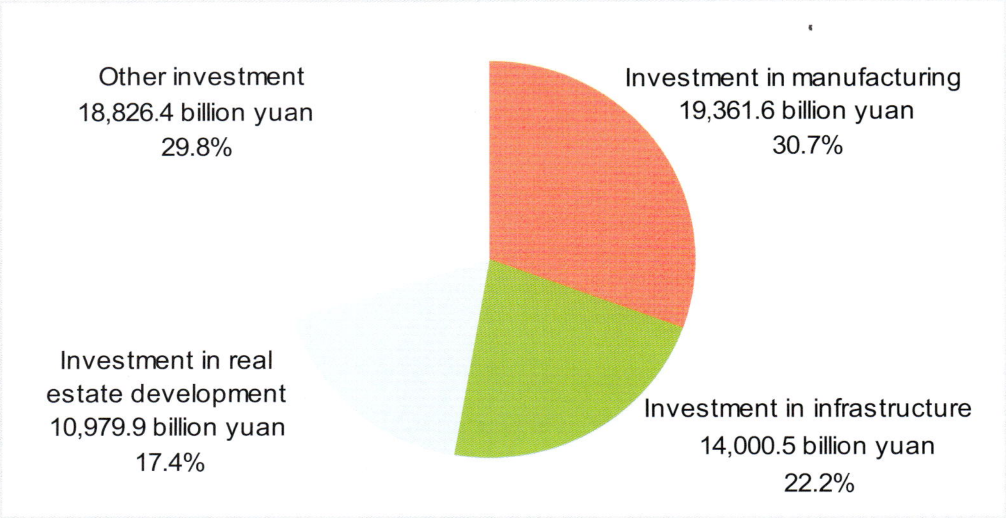

Table 4: Fixed Assets Investment (Excluding by Rural Households) and Its Growth Rates by Sectors in 2017

Sector	Investment (100 million yuan)	Increase over 2016 (%)
Total	**631684**	**7.2**
Agriculture, Forestry, Animal Husbandry and Fishery	24638	9.1
Mining	9209	-10.0
Manufacturing	193616	4.8
Production and Supply of Electricity, Heat Power, Gas and Water	29794	0.8
Construction	3648	-19.0
Wholesale and Retail Trades	16542	-6.3
Transport, Storage and Post	61186	14.8
Hotels and Catering Services	6107	3.9
Information Transmission, Software and Information Technology	6987	12.8
Financial Intermediation	1121	-13.3
Real Estate[31]	139734	3.6
Leasing and Business Services	13304	14.4
Scientific Research and Technical Services	5932	9.4
Water Conservancy, Environment and Public Facilities Management	82105	21.2
Services to Households, Repair and Other Services	2686	2.4
Education	11084	20.2
Health and Social Service	7327	18.1
Culture, Sports and Entertainment	8732	12.9
Public Management, Social Security and Social Organization	7931	-2.0

31. The investment in real estate includes the investment in real estate development, construction of buildings for own use, property management, intermediary services and other real estate investment.

Table 5: Newly Increased Production and Operation Capacity through Fixed Assets Investment in 2017

Item	Unit	Volume
Newly increased power transformer equipment with a capacity of over 220 kilovolts	10000 kilovolt-amperes	24263
New railways put into operation	kilometer	3038
Of which, high-speed railways[32]	kilometer	2182
Extended or new double-track railways put into operation	kilometer	3223
Electrified railways put into operation	kilometer	4583
Length of New and rebuilt highways	kilometer	313607
Of which: Expressways	kilometer	6796
New throughput capacity of berths for over 10,000-tonnage ships	10000 tons/year	24858
New civil transportation airports	-	11
New lines of optical-fiber cables	10000 km	705

In 2017, the investment in real estate development was 10,979.9 billion yuan, up by 7.0 percent. Of this total, the investment in residential buildings reached 7,514.8 billion yuan, an increase of 9.4 percent, that in office buildings was 676.1 billion yuan, up by 3.5 percent, and that in buildings for commercial business was 1,564.0 billion yuan, down by 1.2 percent.

In 2017, 6.09 million housing units were started to be rebuilt in rundown urban areas nationwide. The number of housing units rebuilt in rundown areas was 6.04 million, that the number of public rental housing units built reached 0.82 million. In rural areas of China, among the poverty-stricken households that had their economic status registered at the local governments, 1.525 million[33] of them had witnessed their dilapidated houses rebuilt and renovated in 2017.

32. High-speed railways refer to railways with a maximum operating speed of 200 km/h and above and railways with a maximum operating speed less than 200 km/h but only for high speed trains.

33. It refers to the number of dilapidated houses rebuilt belonging to the poverty-stricken households that had their economic status registered at the local governments by the end of December 2017 which was reported by all provinces (autonomous regions and municipalities).

Table 6: Main Indicators for Real Estate Development and Sales and Their Growth Rates in 2017

Item	Unit	Volume	Increase over 2016 (%)
Value of Investment	100 million RMB	109799	7.0
Of which: residential buildings	100 million RMB	75148	9.4
Of which: 90 square meters and below	100 million RMB	22367	-9.7
Floor space of buildings under construction	10,000 square meters	781484	3.0
Of which: residential buildings	10,000 square meters	536444	2.9
Floor space of buildings newly started	10,000 square meters	178654	7.0
Of which: residential buildings	10,000 square meters	128098	10.5
Floor space of buildings completed	10,000 square meters	101486	-4.4
Of which: residential buildings	10,000 square meters	71815	-7.0
Sales of commercialized buildings	10,000 square meters	169408	7.7
Of which: residential buildings	10,000 square meters	144789	5.3
Funds for investment this year	100 million RMB	156053	8.2
Of which: domestic loans	100 million RMB	25242	17.3
individual mortgage	100 million RMB	23906	-2.0

V. Domestic Trade

In 2017, the total retail sales of consumer goods reached 36,626.2 billion yuan, a growth of 10.2 percent over the previous year. An analysis on different areas showed that the retail sales of consumer goods in urban areas stood at 31,429.0 billion yuan, up by 10.0 percent, and that in rural areas reached 5,197.2 billion yuan, up by 11.8 percent. Grouped by consumption patterns, the retail sales of commodities was 32,661.8 billion yuan, up by 10.2 percent, and that of catering industry was 3,964.4 billion yuan, up by 10.7 percent.

Figure 14 : Total Retail Sales of Consumer Goods 2013-2017

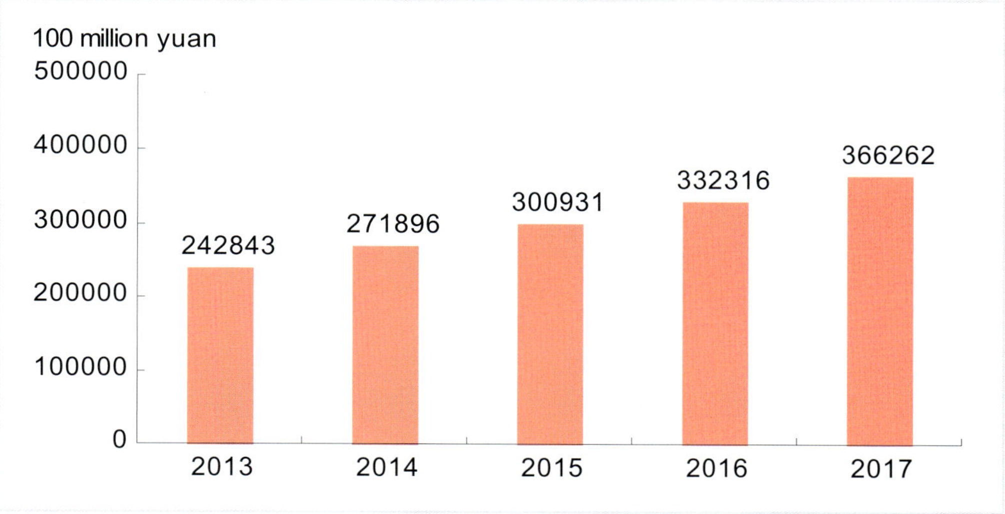

Of the total retail sales of commodities by enterprises above the designated size, the year-on-year growth of sales for grain, oil, food, beverage, tobacco and liquor was up by 9.7 percent, for clothes, shoes, hats and textiles up by 7.8 percent, for cosmetics up by 13.5 percent, for gold, silver and jewelry up by 5.6 percent, for daily necessities up by 8.0 percent, for household appliances and audio-video equipments up by 9.3 percent, for traditional Chinese and western medicines up by 12.4 percent, for cultural and office appliances up by 9.8 percent, for furniture up by 12.8 percent, for telecommunication equipments up by 11.7 percent, for building and decoration materials up by 10.3 percent, for motor vehicles up by 5.6 percent, and for petroleum and petroleum products up by 9.2 percent,

VI. Foreign Economic Relations[34]

The total value of imports and exports of goods in 2017 reached 27,792.3 billion yuan, up by 14.2 percent over the previous year. Of this total, the value of goods exported was 15,332.1 billion yuan, up by 10.8 percent; the value of goods imported was 12,460.2 billion yuan, up by 18.7 percent. The balance of imports and exports (exports minus imports) was 2,871.8 billion yuan, a drop of 473.4 billion yuan over the previous year. The total value of goods imported from and exported to countries along the Belt and Road[35] was 7,374.5 billion yuan, an increase of 17.8 percent over the previous year. Of the total, the value of goods exported was 4,304.5 billion yuan, an increase of 12.1 percent; that of the import was 3,070.0 billion yuan, an increase of 26.8 percent.

Figure 15 : Imports and Exports of Goods 2013-2017

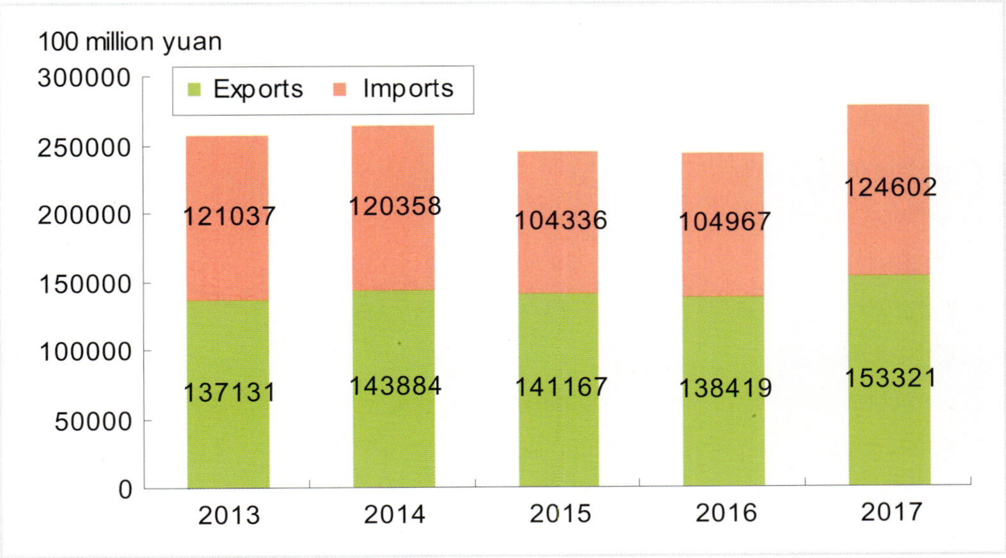

34. Imports and exports of goods and services and foreign investment absorbed are calculated in RMB. Overseas investment and contracted overseas engineering projects are still in US dollar due to technical reasons.

35. The Belt and Road refers to the Silk Road Economic Belt and the 21st Century Maritime Silk Road.

Table 7: Total Value of Import and Export of Goods and the Growth Rates in 2017

Item	Value (100 million yuan)	Increase over 2016 (%)
Total value of import and export of goods	**277923**	**14.2**
Exports	**153321**	**10.8**
Of which: General trade	83325	11.7
Processing trade	51381	8.8
Of which: Mechanical and electronic products	89465	12.1
High & new technology products	45150	13.3
Imports	**124602**	**18.7**
Of which: General trade	73299	23.2
Processing trade	29180	11.3
Of which: Mechanical and electronic products	57785	13.3
High & new technology products	39501	14.1
Trade surplus (exports minus imports)	**28718**	-

Table 8: Main Export Commodities in Volume and Value and the Growth Rates in 2017

Item	Unit	Volume	Increase over 2016 (%)	Value (100 million yuan)	Increase over 2016 (%)
Coal (including lignite)	10000 tons	817	-7.0	75	64.7
Rolled steel	10000 tons	7541	-30.5	3700	3.1
Textile yarns and textile articles	----	—	—	7441	7.4
Clothes and clothing accessories	----	—	—	10656	2.3
Footwear	10000 tons	450	6.5	3269	5.0
Furniture and parts	----	—	—	3385	7.4
Automatic data processing machines and components	10000 sets	154208	-3.1	10710	18.1
Handheld mobiles and car telephones	10000 sets	121087	-4.8	8503	11.3
Containers	10000 units	300	50.6	567	103.2
Liquid crystal display panels	10000 units	193367	1.6	1737	2.3
Motor vehicles	10000 sets	104	43.1	898	27.2

Table 9: Main Import Commodities in Volume and Value and the Growth Rates in 2017

Item	Unit	Volume	Increase over 2016 (%)	Value (100 million yuan)	Increase over 2016 (%)
Cereals and cereals flour	10000 tons	2559	16.4	440	17.2
Soybean	10000 tons	9553	13.8	2688	19.6
Edible vegetable oil	10000 tons	577	4.4	307	11.3
Iron ore and concentrate	10000 tons	107474	5.0	5175	35.0
Aluminum oxide	10000 tons	287	-5.3	75	29.5
Coal (including lignite)	10000 tons	27090	6.1	1536	63.7
Crude oil	10000 tons	41957	10.1	11003	42.7
Petroleum products refined	10000 tons	2964	6.4	982	33.3
Plastics in primary forms	10000 tons	2868	11.5	3284	20.1
Paper pulp	10000 tons	2372	12.6	1039	28.5
Rolled steel	10000 tons	1330	0.6	1027	18.2
Unwrought copper and its alloys	10000 tons	469	-5.2	2115	21.3
Integrated circuits	100 million pieces	3770	10.1	17592	17.3
Motor vehicles	10000 sets	124	15.7	3422	16.3

Table 10: Imports and Exports of Goods by Major Countries and Regions and the Growth Rates in 2017

Country or region	Exports (100 million yuan)	Increase over 2016 (%)	Proportion of the total (%)	Imports (100 million yuan)	Increase over 2016 (%)	Proportion of the total (%)
European Union	25199	12.6	16.4	16543	20.2	13.3
United States	29103	14.5	19.0	10430	17.3	8.4
ASEAN	18902	11.9	12.3	15942	22.8	12.8
Japan	9301	8.9	6.1	11204	16.3	9.0
Hong Kong, China	18899	-0.4	12.3	495	-54.9	0.4
Republic of Korea	6965	12.6	4.5	12013	14.4	9.6
Taiwan, China	2979	12.2	1.9	10512	14.5	8.4
Brazil	1962	35.2	1.3	3974	31.4	3.2
India	4615	19.8	3.0	1107	42.4	0.9
Russia	2906	17.8	1.9	2790	31.0	2.2
South Africa	1004	18.4	0.7	1649	12.1	1.3

The total value of imports and exports of services[36] in 2017 was 4,699.1 billion yuan, up by 6.8 percent. The export value of services was 1,540.7 billion yuan, up by 10.6 percent. The import value of services was 3,158.4 billion yuan, up by 5.1 percent. The deficit of exports minus imports of services was 1,617.7 billion yuan.

The year 2017 witnessed the establishment of 35,652 enterprises (excluding banking, securities and insurance) with foreign direct investment, up by 27.8 percent over the previous year; and the foreign direct investment actually utilized was 877.6 billion yuan (131.0 billion US dollars), up by 7.9 percent, 3.8 percentage points faster than last year. Specifically, there were 3,857 newly established enterprises receiving direct investment from countries along the Belt and Road, up by 32.8 percent; and the foreign capital directly invested in China was 37.4 billion yuan (5.6 billion US dollars). In 2017, the foreign investment actually utilized by high technology manufacturing industry reached 66.6 billion yuan, up by 11.3 percent.

Table 11: Total Value of Foreign Direct Investment (Excluding Banking, Securities and Insurance) and the Growth Rates in 2017

Sector	Enterprises	Increase over 2016 (%)	Actually Utilized Value (100 million yuan)	Increase over 2016 (%)
Total	**35652**	**27.8**	**8776**	**7.9**
Of which: Agriculture, Forestry, Animal Husbandry and Fishery	706	26.5	72	-41.6
Manufacturing	4986	24.3	2259	-1.9
Production and Supply of Electricity, Gas and Water	372	19.6	235	68.1
Transport, Storage and Post	517	21.7	374	13.6
Information Transmission, Computer Service and Software	3169	116.6	1389	157.1
Wholesale and Retail Trades	12283	30.7	770	-23.9
Real Estate	737	95.0	1133	-10.4
Leasing and Business Services	5087	9.9	1125	7.5
Services to Households and Other Services	349	42.5	38	16.0

36. The imports and exports of services are calculated according to the sixth edition of Balance of Payments and International Investment Position Manual (BPM6), and the growth rate is calculated on a comparable basis.

In 2017, the overseas direct investment (excluding banking, securities and insurance) by Chinese investors was 810.8 billion yuan, or 120.1 billion US dollars, down by 29.4 percent over the previous year. Among the investment, Chinese investors directly invested 14.4 billion US dollars in countries along the Belt and Road.

Table 12: Total Value of Overseas Direct Investment (Excluding Banking, Securities and Insurance) and the Growth Rates in 2017

Sector	Overseas Direct Investment (100 million US dollars)	Increase over 2016 (%)
Total	**1201**	**-29.4**
Of which: Agriculture, Forestry, Animal Husbandry and Fishery	22	-25.3
Mining	83	-4.4
Manufacturing	191	-38.4
Production and Supply of Electricity, Heat Power, Gas and Water	32	26.5
Construction	73	37.5
Wholesale and Retail Trades	249	-9.6
Transport, Storage and Post Service	30	-16.9
Information Transmission, Software and Information Technology	103	-49.3
Real Estate	22	-79.6
Leasing and Business Services	349	-17.3

In 2017, the accomplished business revenue through contracted overseas engineering projects was 1,138.3 billion yuan, or 168.6 billion US dollars, up by 5.8 percent. Specifically, the accomplished business revenue from countries along the Belt and Road was 85.5 billion US dollars, an increase of 12 6 percent, accounting for 50.7 percent of the accomplished business revenue through contracted overseas engineering projects. The number of labor forces sent abroad through overseas labor contracts was 0.52 million, up by 5.7 percent.

VII. Transportation, Post, Telecommunications and Tourism

The total freight traffic reached 47.9 billion tons, up by 9.3 percent over 2016. The freight flows were 19,613.0 billion ton-kilometers, up by 5.1 percent. The volume of freight handled by ports above the designated size throughout the year totaled 12.6 billion tons, up 6.4 percent over the previous year, of which freight for foreign trade was 4.0 billion tons, up 5.7 percent. Container shipping of ports above the designated size reached 236.80 million standard containers, up by 8.3 percent.

Table 13: Freight Traffic by All Means of Transportation and Growth Rates in 2017

Item	Unit	Volume	Increase over 2016 (%)
Total freight traffic	**100 million tons**	**479.4**	**9.3**
Railways	100 million tons	36.9	10.7
Highways	100 million tons	368.0	10.1
Waterways	100 million tons	66.6	4.3
Civil aviation	10 000 tons	705.8	5.7
Pipelines	100 million tons	7.9	7.3
Freight flows	**100 million ton-kilometers**	**196130.4**	**5.1**
Railways	100 million ton-kilometers	26962.2	13.3
Highways	100 million ton-kilometers	66712.5	9.2
Waterways	100 million ton-kilometers	97455.0	0.1
Civil aviation	100 million ton-kilometers	243.5	9.5
Pipelines	100 million ton-kilometers	4757.2	13.4

In 2017, the total passenger traffic reached 18.5 billion persons, down by 2.6 percent over 2016, and the passenger flows were 3,281.3 billion person-kilometers, grew by 5.0 percent.

Table 14: Passenger Traffic by All Means of Transportation and Growth Rates in 2017

Item	Unit	Volume	Increase over 2016 (%)
Total passenger traffic	**100 million persons**	**185.1**	**-2.6**
Railways	100 million persons	30.8	9.6
Highways	100 million persons	145.9	-5.4
Waterways	100 million persons	2.8	4.1
Civil aviation	100 million persons	5.5	13.0
Passenger flows	**100 million person-kilometers**	**32812.7**	**5.0**
Railways	100 million person-kilometers	13456.9	7.0
Highways	100 million person-kilometers	9765.1	-4.5
Waterways	100 million person-kilometers	77.9	7.7
Civil aviation	100 million person-kilometers	9512.8	13.5

The total number of motor vehicles for civilian use reached 217.43 million (including 8.20 million tri-wheel motor vehicles and low-speed trucks) by the end of 2017, up 11.8 percent over that at the end of 2016, of which privately-owned vehicles numbered 186.95 million, up 12.9 percent. The total number of cars for civilian use stood at 121.85 million, up 12.0 percent, of which privately-owned cars numbered 114.16 million, up by 12.5 percent.

The turnover of post services[37] totaled 976.4 billion yuan, up 32.0 percent over the previous year. The number of mail delivery, parcel delivery and express delivery reached 3.15 billion, 30 million and 40.06 billion respectively. The revenue from express delivery reached 495.7 billion yuan. The turnover of telecommunication services[38] totaled 2,755.7 billion yuan, up 76.4 percent over the previous year. The newly increased capacity of mobile phone switchboard[39] was 236.46 million lines with the total capacity reaching 2,421.86 million lines. By the end of 2017, there were 1,611.25 million phone subscribers in China, of whom 1,417.49 million were mobile phone users. Mobile phone coverage rose to 102.5 sets per 100 persons. The number of fixed broadband internet users[40] reached 348.54 million, increased by 51.33 million over the previous year. Of this total, fixed fiber-optic broadband internet users[41] amounted to 293.92 million, an increase of 66.27 million. The number of mobile broadband users[42] was 1,131.52 million, an increase of 190.77 million. Mobile internet traffic was 24.6 billion G, up 162.7 percent over the previous year. The number of internet users was 772 million, grew by 40.74 million. Of the total, 753 million were mobile internet surfers[43], an increase of 57.34 million. The coverage of Internet was 55.8 percent nationwide and 35.4 percent in rural areas. Software revenue from software and IT services industry[44] totaled 5,503.7 billion yuan, up 13.9 percent.

37. The turnover of post services is calculated at constant prices of 2010.

38. The turnover of telecommunication services is calculated at constant prices of 2015.

39. The capacity of mobile phone switchboard refers to the number of maximum concurrent users calculated by mobile phone switchboard according to selected calling models and switchboard processing capacity.

40. Fixed broadband internet users refer to those who make registration in the telecommunication enterprises and access the Internet through xDSL, FTTx+LAN, FTTH/0 and other broadband access ways as well as dedicated lines at the end of the reporting period.

41. Fixed fiber-optic broadband internet users refer to those who make registration in the telecommunication enterprises and access the Internet through FTTH or FTT0 at the end of the reporting period.

42. Mobile broadband users refer to those who have records in the billing system and use 3G or 4G network resources at the end of the reporting period.

43. The number of mobile Internet surfer refers to the number of Chinese residents aged 6 and above who connected to and surfed on the Internet via mobile phones in the past six months.

44. Software and IT services industry includes software development, information system integration, IT consulting service, data processing and storage, integrated circuit design and other IT services industry.

Figure 16 : Express Delivery and Growth Rate 2013-2017

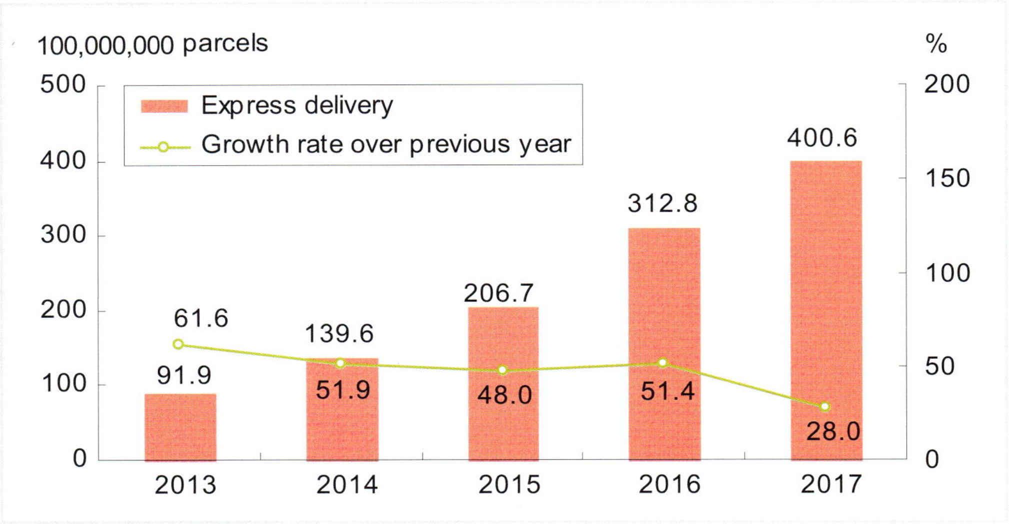

Figure 17 : Year-end Number of Broadband Users 2013-2017

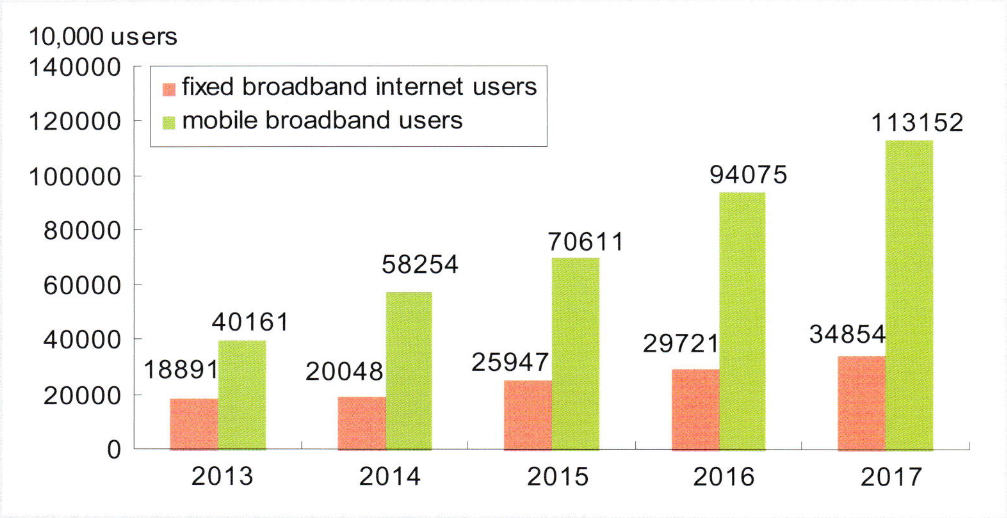

The year 2017 registered 5.0 billion domestic tourists, up 12.8 percent over the previous year. The revenue from domestic tourism totaled 4,566.1 billion yuan, up 15.9 percent. The number of inbound visitors to China totaled 139.48 million, an increase of 0.8 percent. Of this total, 29.17 million were foreigners, up 3.6 percent; and 110.32 million were Chinese compatriots from Hong Kong, Macao and Taiwan, the same level as that of the previous year. Of all the inbound tourists, overnight visitors counted 60.74 million, an increase of 2.5 percent. Earnings from international tourism topped 123.4 billion US dollars, up 2.9 percent. The number of China's outbound visitors totaled 142.73 million, up 5.6 percent. Of this total, 135.82 million were on private visits, an increase of 5.7 percent; and 86.98 million visited Hong Kong, Macao and Taiwan, up by 3.6 percent.

VIII. Financial Intermediation

By the end of 2017, money supply of broad sense (M_2) was 167.7 trillion yuan, reflecting an increase of 8.2 percent. Money supply of narrow sense (M_1) was 54.4 trillion yuan, up 11.8 percent. Cash in circulation (M_0) was 7.1 trillion yuan, up 3.4 percent.

In 2017, the increment of social financing[45] reached 19.4 trillion yuan, or 1.6 trillion yuan more than that in 2016 on a comparable basis. The existing fund of social financing[46] totaled 174.6 trillion yuan at the end of 2017, up by 12.0 percent compared with that at the end of 2016. Savings deposit in Renminbi and foreign currencies in all items of financial institutions totaled 169.3 trillion yuan at the end of 2017, an increase of 13.7 trillion yuan compared with that at the beginning of the year. Of this total, the savings deposit in Renminbi stood at 164.1trillion yuan, an increase of 13.5 trillion yuan. Loans in Renminbi and foreign currencies in all items of financial institutions reached 125.6 trillion yuan, an increase of 13.6 trillion yuan. Of this total, loans in Renminbi were 120.1 trillion yuan, an increase of 13.5 trillion yuan.

Table 15: Savings Deposit and Loans in RMB and Foreign Currencies in All Financial Institutions and Growth Rates at the End of 2017

Item	Year-end figure (100 million yuan)	Increase over 2016 (%)
Savings deposit	**1692727**	**8.8**
Domestic households	651983	7.5
Deposits in RMB	643768	7.7
Domestic non-financial enterprises	571641	7.7
Loans	**1256074**	**12.1**
Domestic short-term loans	411153	8.2
Domestic medium and long-term loans	750894	18.2

Loans in Renminbi from rural financial institutions (rural credit cooperatives, rural cooperation banks and rural commercial banks) totaled 14,982.0 billion yuan by the end of 2017, an increase of 1,560.2 billion

45. The increment of social financing refers to the total funds raised by real economy (domestic non-financial enterprises and individuals) from the financial system over a period of time.

46. The existing fund of social financing refers to the balance of the capital raised by real economy (domestic non-financial enterprises and individuals) from the financial system at the end of a certain period of time (a month, a quarter or a year).

yuan as compared with the beginning of the year. The loans in Renminbi for consumption use from all financial institutions totaled 31,519.4 billion yuan, an increase of 6,471.7 billion yuan. Of the total, short-term personal loans totaled 6,804.1 billion yuan, an increase of 1,872.4 billion yuan, and medium and long-term personal loans reached 24,715.4 billion yuan, an increase of 4,599.3 billion yuan.

Funds raised in 2017 by listed companies through domestic market amounted to 4,083.6 billion yuan, a decrease of 1,224.4 billion yuan from the previous year. Of this total, 419 A-shares completed subscription, raising 218.6 billion yuan worth of capital altogether. The refinancing of A-shares (including public newly issued, targeted placement, right issued, and preferred stock) raised 920.9 billion yuan worth of capital, a decrease of 417.8 billion yuan from 2016. The listed companies financed 2,810.5 billion yuan through issuing bonds (including corporate bonds, convertible bonds, exchangeable bonds and asset-backed securities) on Shanghai and Shenzhen Stock Exchanges, down by 856.3 billion yuan. In 2017, 2,176 companies were newly listed on National Equities Exchange and Quotations[47], raising 133.6 billion yuan, down by 3.95 percent.

In 2017, 5.64 trillion yuan corporate debenture bonds[48] were issued, a decrease of 2.59 trillion yuan over the previous year.

The premium[49] received by the insurance companies totaled 3,658.1 billion yuan in 2017, up 18.2 percent over the previous year. Of this total, life insurance premium amounted to 2,145.6 billion yuan, health and casualty insurance premium 529.1 billion yuan, and property insurance premium 983.5 billion yuan. Insurance companies paid an indemnity worth of 1,118.1 billion yuan, of which, life insurance indemnity was 457.5 billion yuan, health and casualty insurance indemnity 151.8 billion yuan, and property insurance indemnity 508.7 billion yuan.

IX. Households Income and Consumption and Social Security

In 2017, the national per capita disposable income[50] was 25,974 yuan, an increase of 9.0 percent or a real increase of 7.3 percent after deducting price factors. The median[51] of national per capita disposable

---

47. National Equities Exchange and Quotations, also called "the New Over-the-Counter Market", is a national securities exchange established upon approval by the State Council in 2012.

48. Corporate debenture bonds include debt financing instruments of non-financial businesses, enterprise bonds, corporate bonds and convertible bonds.

49. The original premium income received by the insurance companies refers to the premium income from original insurance contracts confirmed by the insurance companies.

50. The reason why the nominal growth rate of national income of residents outpaces that in urban and rural areas is that, in urbanization process, some higher income population in rural areas move to cities and fall into lower income group in urban areas. Their migration lowers the income of urban and rural households. However, the effect of income growth, whether in rural or urban areas, is reflected in the national income growth.

51. The median of per capita income refers to the per capita income of household lied in the middle of all surveyed households which are ranked from low to high (or high to low) based on per capita income level.

income was 22,408 yuan, up 7.3 percent. In terms of permanent residence, the per capita disposable income of urban households was 36,396 yuan, up by 8.3 percent, or a real growth of 6.5 percent after deducting price factors. The median of per capita disposable income of urban households was 33,834 yuan, up by 7.2 percent. The per capita disposable income of rural households was 13,432 yuan, up by 8.6 percent, or 7.3 percent in real terms. The median of per capita disposable income of rural households was 11,969 yuan, up by 7.4 percent. Grouped by income quintile[52], the per capita disposable income of low-income group reached 5,958 yuan, the lower-middle-income group 13,843 yuan, the middle-income group 22,495 yuan, the upper-middle-income group 34,547 yuan and the high-income group 64,934 yuan. The per capita monthly income of migrant workers was 3,485 yuan, increased by 6.4 percent.

The national per capita consumption expenditure was 18,322 yuan, up by 7.1 percent, or a real growth of 5.4 percent after deducting price factors. In terms of permanent residence, the per capita consumption expenditure of urban households was 24,445 yuan, up by 5.9 percent, or 4.1 percent in real terms after deducting price factors. The per capita consumption expenditure of rural households was 10,955 yuan, up by 8.1 percent, or a real growth of 6.8 percent after deducting price factors. The Engel's Coefficient was 29.3 percent, down by 0.8 percentage point over the previous year, with that of urban and rural households standing at 28.6 percent and 31.2 percent respectively.

Figure 18 : National Per Capita Disposable Income and Growth Rates 2013-2017

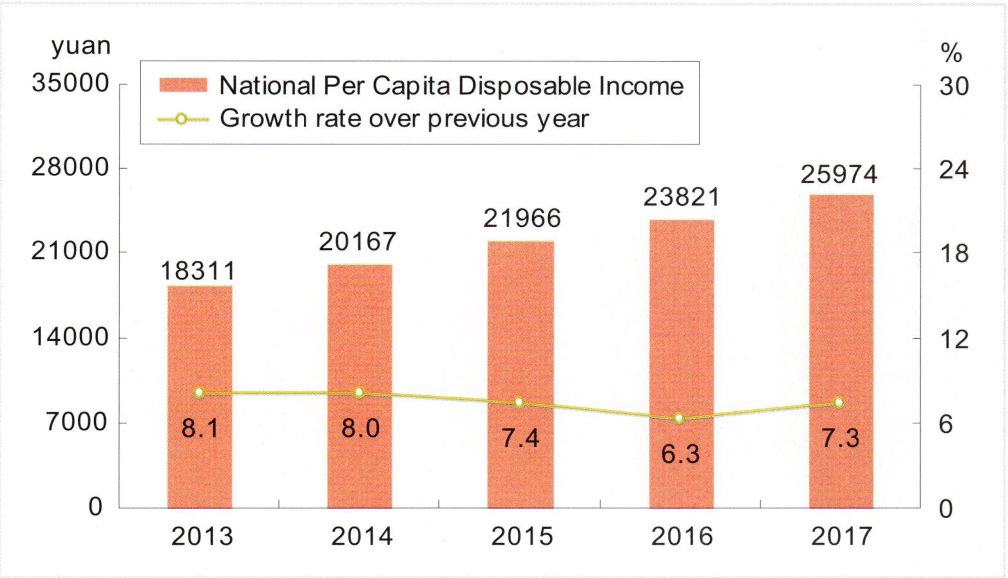

52. The income quintile refers to the five equal partitions of all surveyed households, who are ranked from low to high based on per capita income level. The top 20 percent with the highest income are classified as high-income group, and the other four levels are upper-middle-income group, middle-income group, lower-middle-income group and low-income group.

Figure 19 : National Per Capita Consumption Expenditure and Composition in 2017

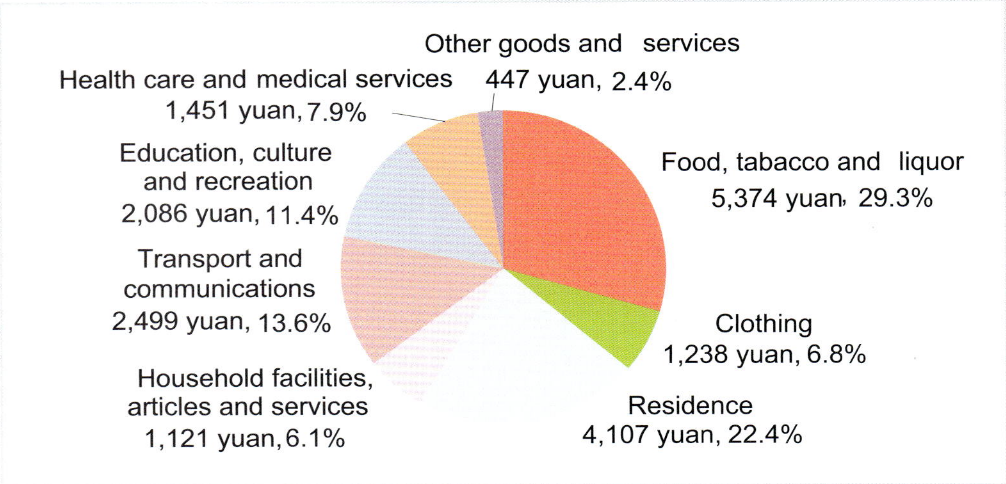

According to the rural poverty line of annual per capita income of 2,300 yuan (at 2010 constant prices), the population in poverty in rural areas numbered 30.46 million by the end of 2017, 12.89 million less[53] than that at the end of 2016. The incidence of poverty[54] was 3.1 percent, 1.4 percentage points lower than that in last year. The per capita disposable income of rural households in impoverished areas[55] was 9,377 yuan, up by 10.5 percent compared with 2016, or 9.1 percent in real terms.

Figure 20 : Year-end Rural Population in Poverty 2013-2017

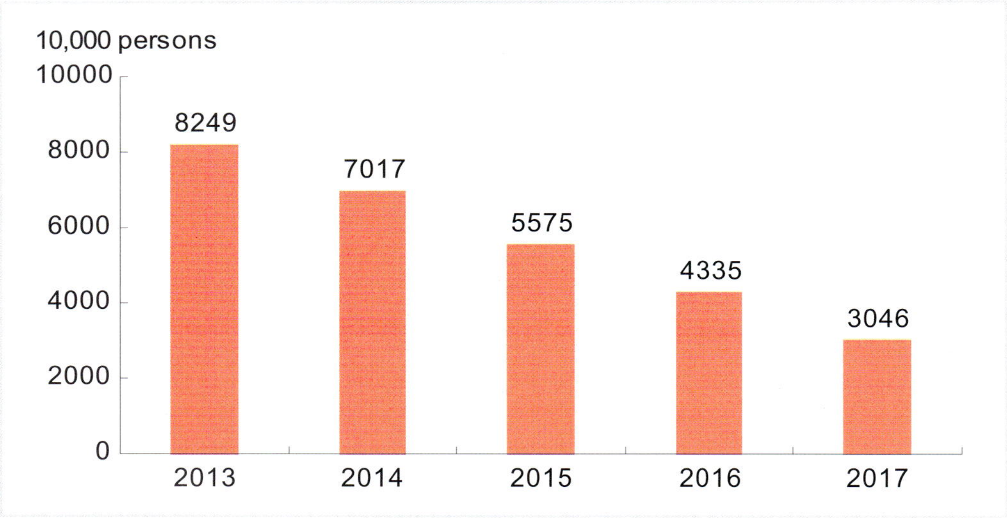

53. The number of people lifted out of poverty equals the population in poverty in the current year minus that in the previous year. It is also equivalent to the population out of poverty minus the population returning to poverty in the current year.

54. The incidence of poverty refers to the proportion of population in poverty to targeted population under survey.

55. Impoverished areas cover contiguous poverty-stricken areas and key counties under national poverty alleviation and development program beyond those areas. There were 832 counties altogether. Since 2017, Aksu prefecture in Xinjiang has also been covered in poverty monitoring.

By the end of 2017, a total of 401.99 million people participated in urban basic pension program for staff and workers, a year-on-year increase of 22.69 million. A total of 512.55 million people participated in basic pension insurance program for urban and rural residents, an increase of 4.08 million. A total of 1,176.64 million people participated in basic medical insurance program, an increase of 432.72 million. Of this total, 303.20 million people participated in basic medical insurance program for staff and workers, an increase of 7.89 million, and 873.43 million people participated in programs for urban and rural residents[56], an increase of 424.83 million. Some 187.84 million people participated in unemployment insurance programs, an increase of 6.95 million. The number of people receiving unemployment insurance payment stood at 2.20 million. A total of 227.26 million people participated in work accident insurance, an increase of 8.36 million. Of this total, 78.07 million were migrant workers, an increase of 2.97 million. A total of 192.40 million people participated in maternity insurance programs, an increase of 7.89 million. Minimum living allowances were granted to 12.64 million urban residents and 40.47 million rural residents, and 4.67 million rural residents living in extreme poverty[57] received relief and assistance. A total of 52.03 million people were financed to participate in basic medical insurance system and medical assistance was granted to 35.36 million cases. National subsidies and allowances were provided to 8.59 million entitled people.

X. Education, Science & Technology and Culture & Sports

In 2017, the post-graduate education[58] enrollment was 2.639 million students with 805 thousand new students and 578 thousand graduates. The general tertiary education enrollment was 27.536 million students with 7.615 million new students and 7.358 million graduates. Vocational secondary schools[59] had 15.925 million enrolled students, including 5.824 million new entrants, and 4.969 million graduates. Senior secondary schools had 23.745 million enrolled students, including 8.001 million new entrants, and 7.757 million graduates. Students enrolled in junior secondary schools totaled 44.421 million, including 15.472 million new entrants, and 13.975 million graduates. The country had a primary education enrollment of

56. The recipients of basic medical insurance for urban and rural residents increased remarkably because the recipients of new type of rural cooperative medical care are now incorporated in the statistics of basic medical insurance for urban and rural residents and the coverage of basic medical insurance is further expanded with the launch of full registration for universal participation in social insurance.

57. Rural residents living in extreme poverty refer to the aged, the disabled and the minor under 16 years of age in rural areas who have no ability to work, no sources of income and no statutory obligors to provide for them, bring them up or support them, or whose statutory obligors have no ability to fulfill their obligations.

58. In 2017, the coverage of new post-graduate students and post-graduate enrollment has changed (part-time post-graduate students were added).

59. Vocational secondary schools include regular specialized secondary schools, adult specialized secondary schools, vocational high schools and skilled workers schools.

100.937 million students, including 17.666 million new entrants, and 15.659 million graduates. There were 579 thousand students enrolled in special education schools, with 111 thousand new entrants and 69 thousand graduates. Kindergartens accommodated 46.001 million children. The number of students graduating from compulsory education reached 93.8 percent of the total enrollment and the gross enrollment rate in senior high schools reached 88.3 percent.

Figure 21 : New Entrants into Education 2013-2017

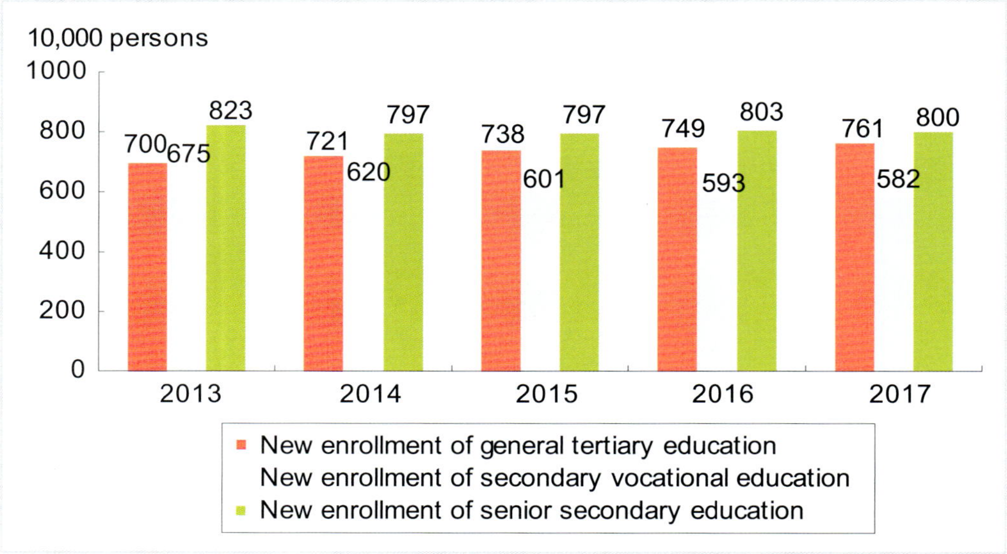

Expenditures on research and development activities (R&D) was worth 1,750.0 billion yuan in 2017, up 11.6 percent over 2016, accounting for 2.12 percent of GDP. Of this total, 92.0 billion yuan was appropriated for fundamental research programs. 1,115 science and technology projects and 42 priority projects were arranged under the national key research and development program. A total number of 454 subjects were arranged under the national science and technology major projects and 43,935 projects were financed by the National Natural Science Foundation. By the end of 2017, there were altogether 503 state key laboratories, 131 national engineering research centers, 217 national engineering laboratories, and 1,276 national enterprise technical centers. The National Fund for Technology Transfer and Commercialization established 5 sub-funds, with the total size reaching 24.72 billion yuan. There were 3,698 thousand patent applications from home and abroad, and a total of 1,836 thousand were authorized. The number of PCT patent applications accepted[60] was 51 thousand. Till the end of year 2017, the number of patents in force was

60. The number of PCT patent applications accepted refers to the number of PCT patent application accepted by the State Intellectual Property Office which acts as the receiving office of PCT patent application. PCT is the abbreviation of Patent Cooperation Treaty, which is a treaty for international cooperation in the field of patents.

7.148 million, of which 1,356 thousand were invention patents from home. The number of invention patents per 10,000 people was 9.8. A total of 368 thousand technology transfer contracts were signed, representing 1,342.4 billion yuan in value, up 17.7 percent over the previous year.

Figure 22 : The Amount of Expenditure on Research and Development Activities(R&D) 2013-2017

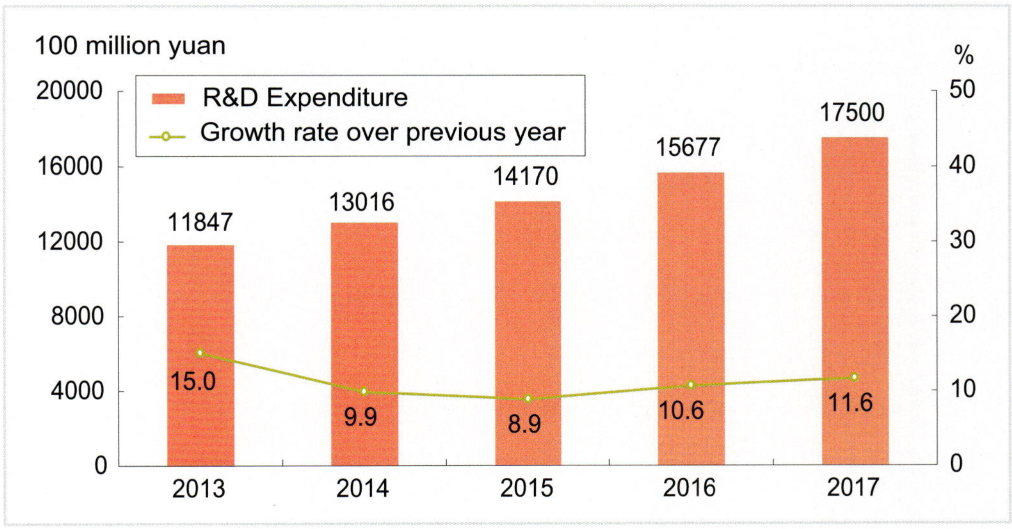

Table16: Number of Patents Application, Patents Authorized and Patents in Force in 2017

Item	Patents (10,000)
Number of patent applications	**369.8**
Of which: domestic	351.3
Of which: for new inventions	138.2
Of which: domestic	123.4
Number of patents authorized	**183.6**
Of which: domestic	170.5
Of which: for new inventions	42.0
Of which: domestic	32.0
Number of patents in force at the end of the year	**714.8**
Of which: domestic	620.4
Of which: for new inventions	208.5
Of which: domestic	135.6

The year 2017 saw 17 times of successful satellite launches. The first high-orbit high throughput satellite Shijian 13 and first large hard X-ray space exploration satellite Insight were launched successfully. Two satellites in Beidou navigation satellite system were lifted off by one rocket for global networking.

Tianzhou-1 Cargo Spacecraft was launched successfully and completed rendezvous and docking mission with Tiangong-2 Space Lab. The quantum satellite Mozi achieved the intended scientific goals. The Dark Matter Particle Explorer Wukong detected an anomaly in electrons. The large passenger aircraft C919 and the amphibious aircraft AG600, codenamed Kunlong made successful maiden flights.

By the end of 2017, there were altogether 35,000 laboratories for product inspection, including 739 national inspection centers. There were 401 agencies for product quality and management system certification, which accumulatively certified products in 140,250 enterprises. There were 4,037 authorized measurement institutions in the year, enforcing compulsory inspection on 83.26 million measurement instruments. A total of 3,811 national standards were developed or revised in the year, including 2,684 new standards.

At the end of 2017, there were 2,054 art-performing groups and 3,217 museums in the cultural system throughout China. A total of 3,162 public libraries received[61] 726.41 million people. There were 3,327 culture centers. Subscribers to cable television programs numbered 220 million, in which 198 million subscribed to digital cable television programs. Radio broadcasting and television broadcasting coverage rates were 98.7 percent and 99.1 percent respectively. A total of 13,310 episodes of 310 TV series and 83,599 minutes of TV cartoons were made in 2017. The country produced 798 feature movies and 172 science, educational, documentary, cartoon and special movies[62]. A total of 36.8 billion copies of newspapers and 2.6 billion copies of magazines were issued, and 9.0 billion copies of books were published. The average number of books possessed per person[63] was 6.49 copies. By the end of the year, there were 4,237 archives in China and 138.06 million documents were made accessible to the public. In 2016, the value added of culture and related industries totaled 3,078.5 billion yuan, up by 13.0 percent over the previous year, accounting for 4.14 percent of GDP, 0.19 percentage point higher than the previous year.

In 2017, Chinese athletes won 106 world championships on 24 sports events and broke 6 world records. Chinese physically-challenged athletes won 160 world championships in 11 international sports competitions. In 2016, the value added of sports industries totaled 647.5 billion yuan, up by 17.8 percent over the previous year, accounting for 0.9 percent of GDP, 0.1 percentage point higher than the previous year.

---

61. The people received by the public libraries refer to the number of people who visit libraries and use library services in the year, including borrowing and reading books, consultation and attending readers' programs.

62. Special movies refers to those using different display modes in terms of projection techniques, equipment and program as compared with the ordinary cinemas, such as IMAX movies, 3D movies, 4D movies, multidimensional movies and full dome movies.

63. The average number of books possessed per person refers to the average number of books published in the year that can be possessed per person in China.

XI. Public Health and Social Services

By the end of 2017, there were 995,000 medical and health institutions in China, including 30,000 hospitals. Of all the hospitals, 12,000 were public, and 18,000 were private. Of the 940,000 medical and health institutions at grass-root level, there were 37,000 township health centers, 35,000 community health service centers, 230,000 clinics and 638,000 village clinics. Of the 22,000 professional public health institutions, 3,482 were disease control and prevention centers and 3,133 were health monitoring institutions. There were 8.91 million health workers in China, including 3.35 million practicing doctors and assistant practicing doctors and 3.79 million registered nurses. The medical and health institutions in China possessed 7.85 million beds, of which, hospitals possessed 6.09 million and township health centers had 1.25 million. The total number of medical visits[64] and hospital discharges[65] in 2017 reached 8.10 billion and 240 million respectively.

Figure 23 : Year-end Number of Health Workers 2013-2017

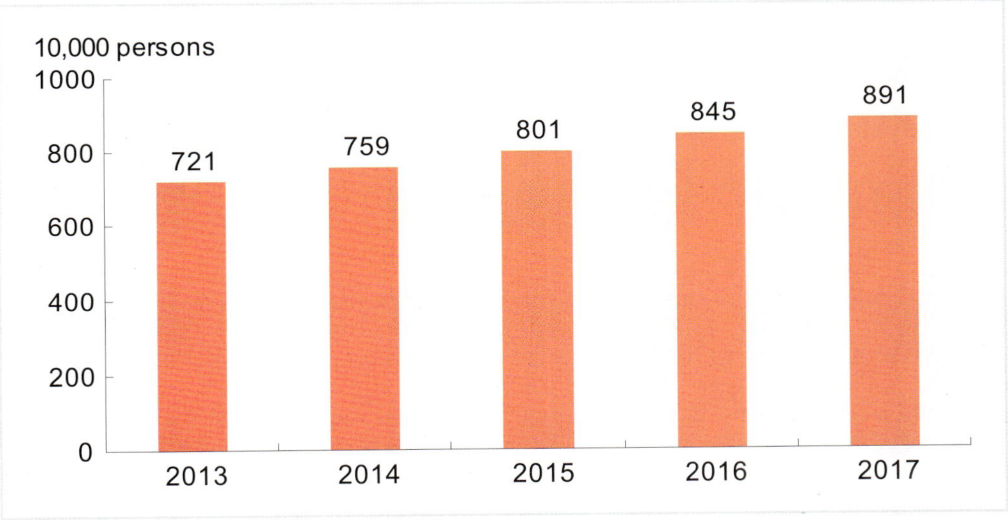

By the end of 2017, there were altogether 32 thousand social welfare institutions providing accommodation, of which 29 thousand were elder-caring organizations and 656 were children caring organizations. The social welfare institutions provided 7.495 million beds[66], of which 7.142 million were for

64. The total number of medical visits refers to the number of people receiving medical services, including outpatient services, emergency treatment, home visits, appointment-based treatment, health check-up of a specific item, and health counseling and guidance (excluding health lectures).

65. The number of hospital discharges refers to the number of inpatients released from hospitals in the reporting period, including those who are discharged from hospitals or transferred to other medical institutions following doctors' advice, discharged from hospitals without doctors' permission, dead or other situations. The number of people who are recovered from family sickbeds is excluded.

66. The beds provided by social welfare institutions include those provided by adoption agencies, aid agencies, community agencies, serviceman recreation habitation and military supply stations etc.

the elderly and 96 thousand were for children. There were 25 thousand community service centers and 139 thousand community service stations.

XII. Resources, Environment and Work Safety

In 2017, the total supply of state-owned land for construction use[67] was 600 thousand hectares, an increase of 16.4 percent over the previous year. Of this total, the supply for mining storage was 120 thousand hectares, up by 1.6 percent; that for real estate[68] was 115 thousand hectares, up by 7.2 percent; and that for infrastructure facilities was 365 thousand hectares, up by 26.1 percent.

The total stock of water resources in 2017 was 2,867.5 billion cubic meters. The annual average precipitation was 640 millimeters. At the end of 2017, the 604 large reservoirs covered by monitoring program in China stored 351.8 billion cubic meters of water, increased slightly over that at the end of last year. With an increase of 0.8 percent over 2016, the total water consumption reached 609.0 billion cubic meters, of which water consumption for living purposes rose by 2.8 percent, for industrial use grew by 0.2 percent, for agricultural use up by 0.6 percent, and for ecological water supplement grew by 1.7 percent. Water consumption for every 10 thousand yuan worth of GDP produced[69] was 78 cubic meters, a decline of 5.6 percent over the previous year. Water consumption for every 10 thousand yuan worth of industrial value added was 49 cubic meters, down by 5.9 percent. Per capita water consumption was 439 cubic meters, up by 0.3 percent.

In 2017, a total of 7.36 million hectares of forests were planted, of which 3.90 million hectares were afforested by manpower, accounting for 53.0 percent of the total. Forest tending areas reached 8.30 million hectares. By the end of 2017, there were 2,750 natural reserves including 463 national ones. A total of 56 thousand square kilometers of eroded land was put under treatment programs.

Preliminary estimation indicated that the total energy consumption in 2017 amounted to 4.49 billion tons of standard coal equivalent, up 2.9 percent over 2016. The consumption of coal increased by 0.4 percent; crude oil, up 5.2 percent; natural gas, up 14.8 percent; and electric power, up 6.6 percent. The consumption of coal accounted for 60.4 percent of the total energy consumption, down 1.6 percentage points over 2016,

67. Total supply of state-owned land for construction use refers to the supply of state-owned land for construction use with the land-used right sold, allocated or leased to units or individuals by the municipal or county governments according to annual land supply plan and in line with relevant laws in the reporting period.

68. Land used for real estate refers to the sum of land used for commercial service and for residence.

69. The consumption of water and energy for producing 10 thousand yuan worth of GDP and water consumption for every 10 thousand yuan worth of industrial value added are calculated at 2015 constant prices.

while clean energy consumption, such as natural gas, hydropower, nuclear power and wind power accounted for 20.8 percent, up 1.3 percentage points. The national energy consumption per 10,000 yuan worth of GDP went down by 3.7 percent. The comprehensive energy consumption per unit caustic soda of key energy-intensive industrial enterprises went down by 0.3 percent, that of per ton cement dropped by 0.1 percent, per ton steel, declined by 0.9 percent, and per ton crude copper, down by 4.8 percent. The standard coal consumption per kilowatt-hour of thermal power generation was decreased by 0.8 percent. The carbon dioxide emission per 10,000 yuan worth of GDP was cut by 5.1 percent.

Figure 24 : The Proportion of Clean Energy Consumption in the Total Energy Consumption 2013-2017

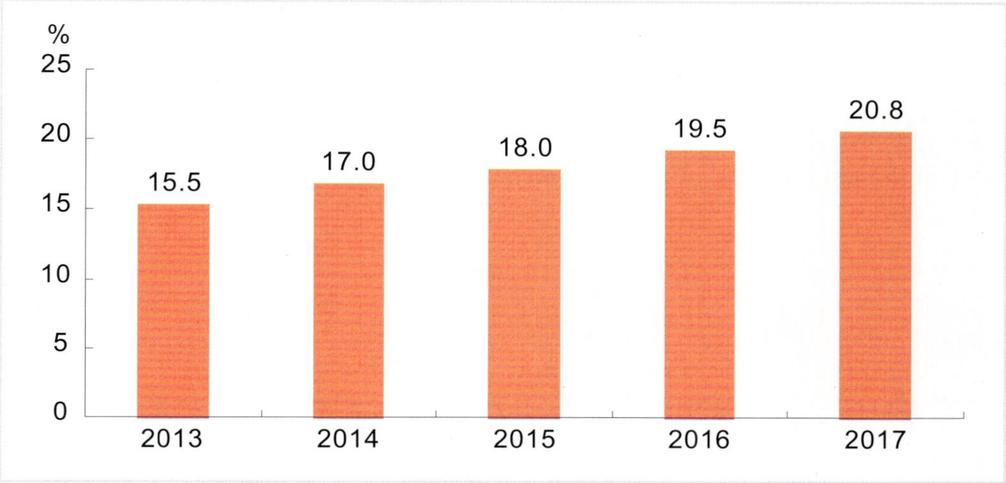

Monitoring of oceanic water quality at 417 offshore monitoring stations indicated that oceanic water met the national quality standard Grade I and II in 67.8 percent of the stations; water quality at 10.1 percent of the stations met Grade III standard; and water of Grade IV or inferior quality was found at 22.1 percent of the stations.

Of the monitored 338 cities at prefecture level and above, 29.3 percent reached the air standard and 70.7 percent failed. The annual average concentration of particulate matter ($PM_{2.5}$) for cities (based on 262 cities failed to reach the standard of annual average concentration in 2015) that failed to meet the standard stood at 48 micrograms per cubic meter, down by 5.9 percent over the previous year.

Of the 323 cities subject to noise monitoring program, 5.9 percent enjoyed fairly good environment, 65.0 percent had good environment, 27.9 percent had fair environment, 0.9 percent had poor environment and 0.3 percent had very poor environment in downtown areas.

The average temperature in 2017 was 10.39℃ , up by 0.03℃ compared with that of the previous year. Typhoon hit China 8 times in 2017.

In 2017, natural disasters hit 18.48 million hectares of crops, of which 1.83 million hectares of crops were demolished. Flood, waterlog and geological disasters caused a direct economic loss of 191.0 billion yuan. Drought caused a direct economic loss of 37.5 billion yuan. Disasters from low temperature, frost and snow made a total direct economic loss of 1.9 billion yuan. Oceanic disasters caused a direct economic loss of 5.8 billion yuan. The country recorded 13 earthquakes with magnitude 5 and over, 11 of which caused disasters, causing a direct economic loss of 14.8 billion yuan. The year 2017 witnessed 3,223 forest fires, with 25 thousand hectares of forests damaged.

The death toll due to work accidents amounted to 37,852 people. Work accidents in industrial, mining and commercial enterprises caused 1.639 deaths out of every 100 thousand employees, down by 3.7 percent over 2016. The road traffic death toll per 10 thousand vehicles was 2.06 persons, down by 3.7 percent. The death toll for one million tons of coal produced in coalmines was 0.106 person, down 32.1 percent.

Data Sources:

In this Communiqué, data of urbanization rate of population with household registration, motor vehicles for civilian use and the traffic accidents are from the Ministry of Public Security; data of newly increased employed people, registered unemployment rate, social security and skilled workers schools are from the Ministry of Human Resources and Social Security; data of foreign exchange reserves and exchange rate are from State Administration of Foreign Exchange; financial data are from the Ministry of Finance; data of qualification rate of manufactured products, quality test and national standard formulation and revision are from General Administration of Quality Supervision, Inspection and Quarantine; data of output of aquatic products are from the Ministry of Agriculture; data of production of timber, forestry and forest fires are from the State Forestry Administration; data of areas with effective irrigation system, water resources and soil erosion are from the Ministry of Water Resources; data of installed power generation capacity and newly increased power transformer equipment with a capacity of over 220 kilovolts are from China Electricity Council; data of new railways put into operation, new double-track railways put into operation, electrified railways put into operation and railway transportation are from China Railway; data of new and rebuilt highways, new throughput capacity of berths for over 10000-tonnage ships, highway transportation, waterway transportation and volume of freight handled by ports are from the Ministry of Transport; data of new civil transportation airports and civil aviation are from the General Administration of Civil Aviation; data of new lines of optical-fiber cables, business volume of telecommunication service, capacity of phone switchboards, phone users, broadband users, mobile internet traffic, internet users, the coverage of internet and software revenue are from the Ministry of Industry and Information Technology; data of housing units rebuilt in rundown areas, public rental housing and dilapidated houses rebuilt belonging to poor rural households that had their economic status registered at local governments are from the Ministry of Housing and Urban-Rural Development; data of imports and exports of goods are from the General Administration of Customs; data of imports and exports of services, foreign direct investment, overseas direct investment, overseas contracted projects and overseas labor contracts are from the Ministry of Commerce; data of pipelines are from China National Petroleum Corporation, China Petrochemical Corporation and China National Offshore Oil Corporation; data of post services are from the State Post Bureau; data of the internet coverage of rural areas are from China Internet Network Information Center; data of tourism are from the National Tourism Administration and the Ministry of Public Security; data of monetary finance and corporate debenture bonds are from the People's Bank of China; data of listed companies are from the China Securities Regulatory Commission; data of insurances are from China Insurance Regulatory Commission; data of urban and rural minimum living allowances, relief and assistance granted to rural residents living in extreme poverty, social services, areas of crops hit by natural disasters, direct economic loss caused by flood, waterlog and geological disaster, direct economic loss caused by drought, direct economic loss caused by low temperature, frost and snow are from the Ministry of Civil Affairs; data of education are from the Ministry of Education; data of national key research and development programs, national science and technology major projects, state key laboratories, national fund for technology transfer and commercialization and technology transfer contracts are from the Ministry of Science and Technology; data of natural science foundation projects are from the National Natural Science Foundation, data of national engineering research centers, national engineering laboratories, enterprise technical centers and carbon dioxide emission per 10,000 yuan worth of GDP are from the National Development and Reform Commission; data of patents are from the State Intellectual Property Office; data of satellite launch are from the State Administration of Science, Technology and Industry for National Defense; data of art-performing groups, museums, public libraries and culture centers are from the Ministry of Culture; data of radio, television, movies, newspapers, magazines and books are from the State Administration of Press, Publication, Radio, Film and Television; data of documents are from the State Archives Administration; data of sports are from the General Administration of Sport; data of physically-challenged athletes are from the China Disabled Persons' Federation; data of health are from the National Health and Family Planning Commission; data of supply of state-owned land for construction use are from the Ministry of Land and Resources; data of natural reserves and environment monitoring are from the Ministry of Environmental Protection; data of average temperature and typhoon are from the China Meteorological Administration; data of direct economic loss caused by oceanic disasters are from the State Oceanic Administration; data of the number of earthquakes and direct economic loss caused by earthquakes are from the China Earthquake Administration; data of work safety are from the State Administration of Work Safety; all the other data are from the National Bureau of Statistics.

In case of any differences between English translation and the original Chinese text, the Chinese edition shall prevail.